INSIDE SECRETS
OF
FINDING A
TEACHING JOB

by Jack Warner and Clyde Bryan with Diane Warner

Park Avenue

Inside Secrets of Finding a Teaching Job

© 1997 Park Avenue Publications
An imprint of JIST Works, Inc.
720 N. Park Avenue
Indianapolis, IN 46202-3490
Phone: 317-264-3720 Fax: 317-264-3709 E-mail: jistworks@aol.com
World Wide Web Address: http://www.jist.com

A companion book to *The Unauthorized Teacher's Survival Guide* by the same authors

See the back of this book for additional JIST titles and ordering information. Quantity discounts are available.

Cover Design by Brad Luther

Printed in the United States of America

2 3 4 5 6 7 8 9   02 01 00 99 98

Library of Congress Cataloging-in-Publication Data
Warner, Jack, 1935-
    The inside secrets of finding a teaching job / by Jack Warner and
Clyde Bryan with Diana Warner.
        p.   cm.
    Includes bibliographical references (p.).
    ISBN 1-57112-079-3
    1. Teachers—Employment—United States.   2. Teaching—Vocational
guidance—United States.   3. Employment interviewing—United States.
    4. Job hunting—United States.   I. Bryan, Clyde, 1935- .
    II. Warner, Diane.   III. Title.
LB1780.W37   1997
    370'.23'73—dc21   97-8988
                                                 CIP

We have been careful to provide accurate information throughout this book, but it is possible that errors and omissions have been introduced. Please consider this in making any career plans or other important decisions. Trust your own judgment above all else and in all things.

ISBN 1-57112-079-3

Dedication

To Beth Bryan,
You were always there for us.
We love you,
Jack, Clyde, and Diane

Acknowledgments

We want to thank Sara Hall, our editor, for her faith in us and for her encouragement and suggestions as we worked on this book. We also want to thank all those who helped us with the research for this book, including those school administrators and members of interview panels who shared their inside secrets with us, so that we could pass them on to you. Our appreciation and thanks also go to the hundreds of teacher candidates and new teachers who participated in our research survey and passed along their best words of advice.

Table of Contents

Chapter 3
Discovering Job Vacancies 67

Chapter 4
Finding the Inside Track 97

Chapter 5
Preparing for the Interview 107

Chapter 6
Sharpening Your Personal Appeal 139

Chapter 7

Your Conduct During the Interview 151

Chapter 8

After the Interview 169

Epilogue 174

Bibliography 175

Appendix of Educator Resource Organizations 177

Introduction

An interesting thing happened during our author tour for our first book, *The Unauthorized Teacher's Survival Guide*: About a third of the people who attended our seminars during a 16-day swing through seven states were unemployed teachers! Although our seminars dealt with the problem of teacher burnout and how to prevent it, we were constantly sought out by unemployed teachers who wanted to know how to land a teaching position in the first place. These teachers were credentialed, full of enthusiasm, and anxious to get started in their teaching careers, and they voiced tremendous frustration at their inability to find jobs.

As we traveled from city to city, frustrated teacher-candidates kept showing up at our seminars and book signings. Even in California, where thousands of new teaching positions have been created through new legislation, there still is fierce competition for "plum" positions in the "plum" districts.

Finally, somewhere along Interstate 5 on the final leg of our tour, it struck us that we needed to write a book about how to find a teaching job in the first place, and it was then the irony hit us: We wrote our second book first!

As we researched this new book, we found out why the job search has become so difficult. For starters, teacher interviews are much more complicated than they used to be. When we first interviewed, for example, we weren't a bit worried about the job market; we merely blitzed our favorite school districts with resumes, then sat back and waited to be called. The interviews themselves were usually rather predictable. They were generally conducted by the site administrator in the principal's office. The questions asked were fairly basic:

"What is your philosophy of education?"

"How would you deal with individual differences in your classroom?"

"How do you handle discipline problems?"

Today, however, the job search process has become far more structured, formal, and intimidating, and the teacher-candidate is faced with a dizzying array of buzz words: *mock interviews, demonstration videos, teacher portfolios, school surveys, networking,* and *role-*

playing. The rules have changed, and teacher-candidates must learn to sell themselves—becoming their own Madison Avenue ad campaigns, so to speak. Suddenly, they find themselves in the roles of publicist, telemarketer, research guru, consummate Internet nerd, networker, critic, and makeover artist. It has become a very complicated process!

Our goal in this book is to simplify the process for you by explaining every step, from application to the interview itself. Best of all, we have included hundreds of fresh, relevant bits of advice gleaned from interviews conducted across the country.

First, we interviewed hundreds of teacher-candidates who are currently out there in the job market, as well as those who have recently survived the job search process and landed a position. We asked them every question we could think of that might help you in your search, including what surprised them most about their interviews, what they wish they had known, and their best advice for those beginning the job search process.

We also picked the brains of administrators, teachers, personnel directors, department chairs, parents, specialists, instructional coordinators, mentor teachers, and others who sit on teacher interview panels. We asked them 16 basic questions, including these:

What impresses you most about a resume or application?

What do you learn from a candidate's body language?

What questions should an interviewee ask and *not* ask during the interview?

What turns you off in an interview?

And what is your best advice for teacher-candidates today?

Talk about "inside secrets," did we ever uncover them!

So sit back, relax, and get the real inside scoop!

1

Increasing Your Marketability

The first step in marketing yourself is to *know yourself*! We've all heard the expression in the world of retail sales, "know your product." In your case, your product is *you*, and you can't sell yourself unless you know your strengths and weaknesses.

Assessing Your Strengths and Weaknesses

If you've just graduated from college, you've probably been so inundated by your hectic academic schedule that you haven't given this subject much thought. But now is the time, and it is imperative that you do so. Why is it so important? Because being aware of your personal strengths and weaknesses is prerequisite to the other steps you must take to market yourself as the top-notch classroom teacher you know you can be. For example, how can you prepare your mission statement, your resume, or your teacher portfolio if you don't *really* know yourself?

Another important reason is this: You will almost certainly be asked to tell about your strengths and weaknesses during your teacher interviews.

From our survey of teacher-applicants all over the United States, we found several questions you can count on being asked at the interview table. These are covered in chapter 5, but you should know this from the start: The one that is *virtually always asked* deals with your strengths and weaknesses. More than likely, it will be put to you in the form of a command rather than a question: "Tell me about your strengths and weaknesses." Think about this for a minute: What is the interviewer *really* asking?

> *Virtually all of the teacher-candidates and newly hired teachers in our survey said they were asked about their strengths and weaknesses in one way or another during their teacher interviews.*

What an interviewer really wants to know is this: "Why should I hire you? What can you do for me? Why should I choose you over the rest of the candidates I am interviewing today?"

So when you're asked about your strengths and weaknesses, you should consider it an open-ended question, a golden opportunity to *sell* yourself—or, as we hear so often these days, a chance to be your own publicist. You need to tout your strengths and minimize any weakness by presenting it as a strength. This is actually quite easy to do, as you will see.

Your Strengths

You have many specific skills and positive character traits; some are tangible, some intangible.

Your tangible skills include those related to the teaching profession—including your ability to teach on the elementary or secondary level—and specific skills, such as your ability to work with bilingual or gifted children. Most of these job-related skills are listed on your application and resume and are already familiar to the interview panel. However, you may have many other tangible skills that are not shown on your resume but that will greatly enhance your chances of being hired.

For example, you may have coached Little League, taught swimming lessons, or been a camp counselor. Or perhaps you worked your way through college by tutoring struggling students. These all require skills that are transferable to the teaching profession. Your personal hobbies often involve transferable skills, as well: For example, you may enjoy working with puppets, playing the guitar, surfing the 'Net, playing chess, sewing, or crafting.

By the way, if you're having trouble identifying your skills, the next time you're at the library check out a copy of *What Color Is Your Parachute?* by Richard Bolles. The book will help you uncover your hidden skills and talents, and by the time you're through, you'll be oozing with self-esteem.

Next, we come to your intangible skills. These could also be called "invisible" skills, because they have to do with your personality, your character, and your ability to get along with others. Are you patient? Caring? Trustworthy? Loyal? Responsible? Self-disciplined? Honest? Positive? Do you have a sense of humor? Do you get along well with others? Do you have a strong work ethic? Do you really *love* children? Are you *excited* about becoming a teacher? Are you a dependable, punctual person? Do you enjoy working on a team? Do you get a charge out of motivating students? If so, let the interview panel know: They may never know unless you tell them!

And how about your leadership qualities? Are you a good organizer? Then *tell* the interviewer so! And be *specific*. For example, tell about the time you worked with a group of parents to coordinate a fund-raiser, or how you initiated a neighborhood watch program in your subdivision.

Remember, the interview panel is looking for reasons to hire you, reasons why you're the one they want on their staff.

"Be prepared to give the answer that wants *to* be heard."

—An ESL/ English teacher in Vancouver, British Columbia

Why are these intangible qualities so important? Because the interview committee already *knows* your academic background, including your college major and minor, what credentials you hold, and what you're qualified to teach. You wouldn't have been called for an interview in the first place if you didn't fit their needs in a professional sense. What they really want to know about—and what they can find out only during a personal interview—are your intangible strengths: those positive qualities that say you're an enthusiastic, likable, dependable person.

Be prepared to give specific examples of your strengths, if asked. It's also a good idea to put one at the very top of your list, just in case you're asked, "What is your one greatest strength?" Unless you've thought about it ahead of time and rehearsed your response, you may be caught off guard.

If you tell the panel that your greatest strength is your dependability, for example, be prepared to explain how you're always the first one in the parking lot in the morning because you don't like to be late for work. If your greatest strength is that you relate well to kids, tell them how much fun you had teaching swimming lessons last summer and how well you got along with the children and their parents.

A word of caution: Don't get *too* carried away with the details; make your case and move on. In 30 seconds to a minute you can, with practice, build a very strong case for yourself when asked about your greatest strength. Don't beat it to death!

Your Weaknesses

> *"You have about 30 minutes to sell yourself to the interview committee, to make them want to hire you. This is your one and only chance, so be prepared!"*
> —An elementary school principal in St. Louis, Missouri

Once you've told the panel about your strengths, expect to be asked about your weaknesses. Fortunately, your weaknesses or "limitations" don't have to work against you at the interview table. You "know your product" and the limitations you may have, but don't be too quick to plead guilty to a weakness if you can turn it around and convert it into something that will make you look good.

When you're faced with the question, "Tell us about your weaknesses," don't go on the defensive and immediately begin to explain how you don't like to teach science because it's always been difficult for you, or that you never quite had the interest in it as you have in other areas, blah, blah, blah. Right away you've turned the committee off and they've heard just about all they want to hear on the subject.

The fact that multi-subject teachers feel more prepared to teach some subject areas than others is a given, so try to stay away from specific academic subject areas or job-related classroom skills. Instead, talk about your most "angelic" weakness, one that can be turned into positives. Here are some examples:

Don't say:

"I'm a poor manager of my time."

Do say:

"Sometimes I have so many good ideas and things I want to accomplish with the kids that I get frustrated when I run out of time."

Don't say:

"I'm such a nit-picker that it gets in the way of my progress."

Do say:

"I'm too demanding on myself—too much of a perfectionist."

Don't say:

"I never seem to be able to reach my goals."

Do say:

"My expectations for myself and my students are high, and with time constraints I feel I don't always reach my goals."

Don't say:

"I have very little patience with people who waste my time."

Do say:

"When working or planning with others, I sometimes get frustrated when the time is not used efficiently . . . too much bird-walking . . . too many rabbit trails. I have had to teach myself to be patient."

Whatever you do, don't confess to a weakness in classroom management or in a certain subject area—you will only be digging a hole for yourself! Instead, take one of your most "innocent" and "harmless" weaknesses and turn it into a positive.

Prepare a Mission Statement

Now that you've assessed your strengths and weaknesses, you're in a perfect frame of mind to work on your mission statement. What is a mission statement?

Professionally speaking, a mission statement is what has been called your "philosophy of education," "career statement," or "vision statement." It seems that everyone has a mission statement these days: Individuals, families, corporations, associations, and organizations all proudly display them. These mission statements usually include an all-encompassing purpose and vision for the person's or family's life, the association's policies and goals, or the corporation's philosophy of doing business, interacting with their employees, serving the public, and so forth.

A teacher's mission statement pertains specifically to the teaching profession. If you take it seriously and write it thoughtfully, it can be one of the most powerful and significant things you ever compose. It will become a compass to guide you for the rest of your professional life.

A mission statement typically includes some or all of these components:

> *"The only limit to the realization of tomorrow will be our doubts of today."*
> —Franklin Delano Roosevelt

✓ **Who you are:** Your strengths, skills, talents, and personality traits
✓ **Your guiding principles:** Your beliefs, standards, and character traits
✓ **Your passion to teach:** Why you are passionate about teaching, and how your strengths and beliefs will benefit you professionally
✓ **Your vision as a teacher:** Where you plan to be professionally five or ten years from now, including your goals for professional growth, future credentials, or certificates
✓ **Your legacy:** How you hope to make a difference by positively affecting the lives of others

Here is an example:

One Teacher's Mission Statement

My mission is:

"To use my creative skills, particularly in the fields of art and music, to enhance and inspire the lives of my students.

To dedicate my heart of compassion to the teaching profession, always nurturing and encouraging my students.

To create a classroom with a challenging environment so

that every student will reach his or her maximum potential intellectually and socially.

To share my optimism and generally sunny disposition with everyone I meet, especially my students, their parents, and my peers.

To continue to grow as a teacher and as a person, taking advantage of professional classes and seminars, eventually earning my administrative credential.

To value my students, to show them respect, and to build their self-esteem in some way every day. When my students are my age, I want to be the teacher who stands out in their memories because they knew I cared."

Although brief, this mission statement is quite powerful. Your statement can be longer and more detailed, however, if you include more specifics. Here are a few examples of details you might include:

- ✓ An experience or person who motivated you to go into education
- ✓ What you specifically hope to accomplish within your discipline
- ✓ Why you value the American family, including your own, and how you plan to incorporate these values into your teaching
- ✓ Your philosophies of teaching children and managing your classroom
- ✓ How you plan to deal with your students' individual differences
- ✓ Rewarding student teaching experiences you had that you hope to repeat with your own class of students
- ✓ Your belief that *every* child, regardless of socioeconomic or ethnic background, deserves the same quality instruction and challenging learning experiences
- ✓ Your belief that a teacher should be a role model

- ✓ Why every student should be given the opportunity to utilize technology
- ✓ Why each student should be challenged to develop critical thinking skills and become a lifelong learner
- ✓ Your belief that students should be stimulated and motivated so they will want to stay in school
- ✓ Why children should be treasured, respected, nurtured, praised, and encouraged
- ✓ Your desire to be a team player, willing to contribute to the extra activities of the school and the community

> *"Be well prepared in self-reflection, in terms of what you personally believe about teaching and what you wish to accomplish within your discipline."*
>
> —*P.E. teacher in Charlottesville, Virginia*

- ✓ Why your students should be taught a sense of responsibility for themselves, each other, and for the earth's resources
- ✓ Your desire to find a school and staff that nurture a rich multicultural environment for learning
- ✓ Why students should be guided firmly, but with kindness and fairness
- ✓ Your high expectations for your students—and your patience to help them reach those expectations
- ✓ Your desire to develop the whole person, so your students will be prepared not only for college but to enter the workforce and have families of their own
- ✓ Your goal to have each one of your high school seniors graduate with the abilities to live productive lives, to love themselves and others, and to continue to have a love for learning

These are just a few examples to get your creative juices flowing. What do you truly believe? What drives you to become a teacher? Only you know where your passions lie, which is why every mission statement is different. There is no set formula, and we can't dictate what you should say.

> "A teacher affects eternity; no one can tell where his influence stops."
> —Henry Adams

Whether your mission statement is long or short, however, you will find it an invaluable tool for several important reasons.

First, it will clarify things in your own mind: your strengths, your passions, your goals, and your future.

Second, it will help you see exactly where you've come from, where you are now, and where you're headed in the years to come. Although you may not realize it, this will be a tremendous help as you sell yourself in the job market. For example, it will give you direction as you write your resume and your cover letter, create your teacher portfolio, conduct your school surveys, do your networking, and interact during your job interviews.

And maybe, best of all, you'll be ready when they ask the inevitable question during the interview: "Tell us about yourself."

Extras Count

It's safe to say that anything "extra" you can add to your resume and portfolio to increase your marketability should be included: your talents, experiences, skills, and positive character traits. The idea, of course, is to make you stand out above the rest.

Let's assume that in marketing your product, you've included all of these things, and you have a great resume (we'll cover resume writing in chapter 2). Let's also assume you had a very encouraging, successful student teaching experience, and you have even gained valuable teaching experience through substitute teaching. These are all pluses, but there may be many other applicants out there who are offering essentially the same package.

Yes! I'll Pursue That Extra Credential or Certificate!

So, everything else being equal, it may be the teacher with the extra certificate or credential who lands the job. We understand, having been down that road ourselves a few times, that the extra credential or certificate is not easy to come by. More time, more work, more money. And maybe it's impossible for you to pursue one at this time. What we've learned, however, not only from teachers currently in the job market but also from those who sit on interview panels, is that having a second credential or certificate makes a candidate more attractive to the school district.

In our survey, 3 percent of the teacher candidates considered themselves bilingual, and 9 percent had some type of special ed. credential.

A credential or certificate in one of these three areas can greatly enhance your chances of getting a job:

1. **Bilingual Education Certificate of Competence** (depending, of course, on the number of Limited-English-Proficient or language-minority students in the district and how committed the district is to bilingual education)

2. **Speech/Language Credential**

3. **Special Education Credential**

The availability of jobs in these areas often far exceeds the supply of credentialed candidates. And many of the teacher-applicants we talked with said they were asked by interview panels if they would be willing to pursue an extra credential or certificate if hired; 43 percent of these applicants said they would.

If you are still in college and your long-range goal is to work in speech therapy, special education, bilingual education, or some other specialty, you may want to pursue the extra credential now, in conjunction with your teaching credential. That way, you'll have a leg up on your competition, making your product more attractive during the hiring process.

If, however, you have completed your credential work and you don't already have an extra credential or certificate, we recommend that you agree to pursue one if you are asked to do so. This question may come up at the interview table. If you go into the interview with a ready, positive response, it will put you in better stead than those who hesitate at the idea.

> *In our survey, 43 percent of teacher-candidates were willing to pursue an additional teaching credential or certificate in order to be hired.*

One last comment on this subject: If you are looking for a position in a state or district with a heavy concentration of language minority students, you may soon find that the extra certificate in bilingual education is almost mandatory. And if you are in one of the increasing number of states with strong commitments to bilingual education, you would also do well to pursue this as a second certificate.

In fact, California now has *two* bilingual ed. certificates: the Cross-Cultural, Language, and Academic Development (CLAD) and the Bilingual Cross-Cultural, Language, and Academic Development (BCLAD). Many education majors in California are now pursuing their CLAD or BCLAD concurrently with their regular teaching credential. Your state may have similar certificates available, especially if the philosophy of bilingual ed. is important at the state level. You should also find out if there is any legislation of this kind pending in your state.

The main difference between the CLAD and BCLAD, by the way, is that, in order to pursue the BCLAD, you must have a "language of emphasis" other than English—and you must be tested on your proficiency in that language in speaking, listening, reading, and writing. (In other words, you must be fluent.) A CLAD certificate will definitely help you land a teaching position. And the BCLAD will open doors for you wherever there are large populations of language minority children.

Here are some other excellent areas to consider for an additional credential or certificate:

- ✓ Special Education
- ✓ Vocational Education
- ✓ Computer Education
- ✓ English as a Second Language (ESL)
- ✓ Library Science (or Educational Media)
- ✓ Counseling and Guidance
- ✓ Administration (after you have some teaching experience)

Whether you're a multiple-subject or a single-subject teacher, you should consider adding that extra certificate or credential; it's the closest you'll come to a sure thing, a way to land a position in a tight job market.

Following are some sample job announcements in three of the specialization areas listed above:

Pacific Coastal Unified School District
1874 COASTAL DRIVE
Pleasant Beach, CA 93401
Telephone: (805) 555-1100

POSITION: SPECIAL EDUCATION TEACHER—One part-time (2 Periods or .4 FTE) temporary position for an Itinerant Resource/Special Education teacher for Pleasant Beach High for the 1996-97 school year.

QUALIFICATIONS REQUIRED: Current California Special Education Credential. Special Day Class experience at secondary level. Must verify competency in English by either having passed CBEST or by passing District examination, if hired for the position.

DESIRABLE: Resource Specialist Certificate of Competence. Demonstrated competence as *a* Resource Specialist; Collaborative experience in regular education class; Current assessment practices in special education; Certificate of competence for bilingual and/or bicultural instruction; Knowledge of instructional strategies, including teaching to an objective and using sound principles of learning; Ability to use effective classroom management techniques; Knowledge of applicability of student learning styles information; Knowledge of word processing.

SALARY AND WORK YEAR: Placement on teachers' salary schedule and teachers' work year. Start Date: ASAP.

APPLICATION PROCEDURE

It is the applicant's responsibility to provide the following - An incomplete application will <u>disqualify</u> an applicant:

☞ A completed District application form.
☞ A completed District supplemental application form.
☞ Letters of reference from superintendents, principals, supervisors and/or student teaching master teachers OR Placement File.
☞ Copy of Credential(s) or explanation of credential status. (Explain in detail on front of employment application).

ALL APPLICATIONS WILL BE ACCEPTED UNTIL POSITION IS FILLED; INTERVIEWS WILL BE SCHEDULED UPON APPLICATIONS BEING RECEIVED AND EVALUATION PROCESS COMPLETED.

All applications will be carefully screened on the basis of job-related criteria. Applicants deemed to be most qualified will be contacted for an interview. After selection has been made, all applicants will be notified.

In compliance with Federal laws all new employees must prove their United States citizenship or prove their legal alien status. Specific documents pertaining to this requirement must be provided upon offer of employment.

WE ARE AN EQUAL OPPORTUNITY/ AFFIRMATIVE ACTION EMPLOYER.

Pacific Coastal Unified School District has adopted policies
for non-smoking and tobacco-free schools/facilities

va\special.edu
96-97/29

JOHNSON COUNTY OFFICE OF EDUCATION
Mary E. Carpenter, Ed.D., County Superintendent of Schools
101 Oakfield Drive · Springfield, Illinois · 62723
(217) 555-0001 · FAX (217) 555-0012

POSITION ANNOUNCEMENT

September 25, 1996

TO: Placement Offices and Candidates

FROM: Human Resources, Johnson County Office of Education

SUBJECT: ANNOUNCEMENT OF A TEMPORARY POSITION FOR
1996-97 SCHOOL YEAR

> **POSITION:** **Speech and Language Specialist**
>
> **LOCATION:** Johnson County
>
> **SALARY RANGE:** $24,890 to $54,300
>
> **CLOSING DATE:** October 23, 1996

MINIMUM REQUIREMENTS:

Education: Bachelor's or Master's degree.

Experience: Experience as a public school speech therapist desirable.

Credential: Speech and Language credential

DUTIES AND RESPONSIBILITIES:

Under the direction of the Program Manager, Speech Program:

- Identifies children with communicative and speech disorders through screening and testing.
- Implements a specialized speech correction program designed to remediate children's speech problems.
- Maintains a close, participative, working relationship with school staff, parents, and administration.
- Prepares goals and objectives for students placed in the speech program.
- Provides clinical individualized assistance with speech and language.

Speech & Language Specialist   **DEADLINE: 10/23/96**

HUMAN RESOURCES
An Equal Opprortunity Employer

WINFIELD UNION SCHOOL DISTRICT

Job Announcement

September 25, 1996

CERTIFICATED POSITION
  5th Grade Teacher - Bilingual Class

- Harper Valley Elementary School
- Beginning Salary Range: Pet WETA Salary Schedule
- Number of Annual Work Days: 185
- Health Benefit Package as Identified in Contract

QUALIFICATIONS
- Multiple Subjects Teaching Credential
- Bilingual Certificate of Competence LDS Certificate or willing to pursue language development certificate.
- Bilingual (Spanish Speaking) Preferred
- A copy of valid credential must be attached to your application

FILING DEADLINE

- October 4, 1996

APPLICATION PROCEDURE-:

Current WUSD Certificated Employees may submit letter of interest in lieu of application package.

Candidates are invited to submit the following:

Application
Letter of Introduction
Resume
Placement file or 3 letters of reference
Copy of Multiple Subjects credential
Copy of Language Certificate

To the Attention of:

Peggy Chafin, Ed.D.
District Superintendent
564 East 13th Street
Winfield, New Jersey 08640
(609) 555-2121

Contact Carol at 555-2121 for information

Applicants who fail to submit <u>all required information</u> will not be considered for employment.

AN EQUAL OPPORTUNITY EMPLOYER

Yes! I'll Teach Any Grade Level!

Another extra you can list to make yourself more attractive to a school district is to be flexible about which grade level or subject area you will teach. If you are willing to teach any one of three or four grades or subjects, for example, you are much more useful to the district, which significantly improves your marketability.

Your willingness to be flexible increases your marketability in another important way: As we've already seen, interview committees often ask questions that have more than one purpose. If they ask if you are willing to teach grade levels other than the one for which you are interviewing, it may be because they have filled that particular position—but they have another.

They may also be trying to determine how flexible you are. You see, school districts are looking for teachers who are team players and who have great attitudes. They may not actually need you to teach at another grade level at all. They may simply be testing you to see if you are willing to fit in with *their* plans and meet *the district's* needs, as they change from year to year.

Good administrators do not hire for the here and now; they hire for the long haul. Perhaps a community is growing because a new company is relocating there, creating 3,000 job openings. A good school administrator looks at that community and sees the need for many new teachers. On the other hand, perhaps a company with 500 employees plans to move elsewhere in two years. A wise administrator wants teachers on board who can teach multiple grades or more than one subject, because the school's enrollment is likely to decline.

Birth rates also come into play. Although the number of children born annually may be static in any given community, there will always be occasional peaks and valleys in the birth rate. As large or small classes work their way through the school system, administrators need personnel who are *flexible*.

If you can convince an interview panel that you're enthusiastic about teaching a variety of age groups within their school or district, what they read is this: "Hey, this candidate has the same qualifications as the others we've interviewed today, but this one is willing to fit in where we can use him best. This kind of flexible attitude is exactly what we're looking for."

In our survey, 71 percent of the teacher-candidates were willing to accept positions at any grade level or in any subject for which they were qualified.

Look at it this way: Most teacher credential programs require student teachers to teach at two different grade levels anyway, so you've undoubtedly had the experience, and the interview committee knows this. But whether you're interviewing for a position at the elementary, middle school, or secondary level, the very fact that you don't balk at the possibility of teaching several grade levels up or down from your ideal will impress them.

If you're *determined* to hold out for a fifth- or sixth-grade position, or if your heart is set on teaching *only* Honors English to bright high school seniors, maybe you should try to take the interviewers' perspective for a moment. They might respect your desire to hold to your ideals. Or the next interviewee in the door may get the job instead of you because of his or her flexibility (sometimes interpreted as *attitude*).

It might seem like a small thing, but if you really want to stand out from the rest and increase your chances of being hired, give this idea some serious thought.

Yes! I'll Teach at Any School!

If you're interviewing in a *great* district where you would *love* to teach at *any* school, and you're offered a position that fits in with your goals and vision for your future in education, it's an easy decision to make. *Sign the contract,* regardless of school placement.

But what if you're interviewing with a district where only one or two schools are attractive to you—and you're not crazy about the idea of teaching at any of the others? If you're offered a position in this district and they ask if you'd be willing to teach at *any* school, what should you do?

Before you answer that question, remember that they *might* be checking out your flexibility, your willingness to fit in where their needs dictate. If you're willing to go to any school, you become much more valuable than another candidate who's holding out for only one or two schools. *Don't bump yourself out of the running for lack of flexibility.*

If you're sincere in your job search—if you really need a job—you must be willing to accept a first-year position at any school within a district. Then, in a year or two, if you still prefer another campus and a position opens up, you can apply for a lateral transfer. If you've done a good job, chances are you'll be given preference over someone new to the district.

If you're determined to hold out for one certain school within the district, you may be passing up a chance to be hired at all. You see—and this is one of our "inside secrets"— other tenured teachers within the district may be applying for a lateral transfer to the position, as well, which means you're competing against one of their own. But, you say, this leaves another vacancy open, doesn't it? Exactly! But you won't be considered for it unless you agree *at the time of the interview* to accept any vacancy that opens up.

Look at it as a game of musical chairs. When the music stops, someone is left without a chair. Kind of a sinking feeling. Embarrassing, too. But your job search is not a game. This is your career. And though we believe you should *not* accept a position in September you wish you could leave in November, we also believe you shouldn't be *too* selective. (The key word is *too.*)

Of course you should try for the plum, that ideal job that is at the top of your wish list. But there comes a time when good judgment and conventional wisdom dictate taking a position if offered, then looking at making a change or applying for a transfer a few years down the road.

We talked with many teacher-candidates who said their interviews went extremely well, but they were never offered a position, and they didn't know why. It could be they were holding out for a certain school, and their inflexibility killed their chances of being hired.

If you do accept a position at a school other than the one you wanted, here is one word of caution: Be sure you put your heart and soul into it, as you'll be expected to do. In fact, throughout your first year, give yourself an attitude check occasionally to be sure you're not just "riding this one out" until something better comes along. More than likely, you'll find that you're working with a good group of colleagues, and you may just discover that you're really happy right where you are. As we look back over our careers, we find some of our most rewarding experiences came from the most difficult, challenging situations. Adversity sometimes brings out the best in us.

On the other hand, if after a year or two at the first school you decide to apply for a transfer within the district, at least you will have established yourself and probably received your tenure. Also, you'll be much more knowledgeable about the schools in the district and where you might like to go next. There's definitely stress involved in making a move of any kind, but if you think you would be happier at a different school, it may be worth the stress.

Just remember that in education, as every other profession, you don't always start out exactly where you think you want to be. Lateral moves can come later. You could call that playing the "seniority card," but it's often the road you must take to get to your ideal position and school.

While we're on the subject of being flexible about where you'll teach, there are a couple more options to consider—

neither of which should be considered a second best or "only a place to start my career."

Private Schools

If there are private schools in your area, do some calling and include them when you conduct your school surveys (we'll discuss these in chapter 3). You will discover many types of private schools, including military academies, church or religious schools, day-care centers, nonsectarian independent schools, and college preparatory boarding schools.

> *Fifty percent of the teacher-candidates in our survey pursued each and every job opportunity, even though the positions weren't exactly what they wanted.*

Some of these require their teachers to have state teaching credentials and some do not. Also, church schools and those affiliated with religious denominations may expect their teachers to agree with their religious beliefs. A teacher's commitment to these beliefs may even be included in the teaching contract.

Private schools typically are unique in several ways, and there are advantages as well as disadvantages to teaching in one of them. One of the advantages is that they usually boast a smaller student-to-teacher ratio. Many teachers find themselves more suited to a private school setting, especially if they agree with the school's theology or philosophy. Further, you'll often find a close-knit camaraderie among the students, staff, and parents at private schools that a public school may not have.

The most obvious downside is often salary, as private schools usually aren't as well-funded as public schools. This factor alone keeps many teachers from considering a private school, even though they might otherwise enjoy the private school experience. If the idea of teaching at one of these schools sounds attractive to you, check it out.

Private school teaching vacancies may be listed with your college placement office or in the classified section of your local newspaper. The best sources, however, are the schools themselves; contact each one to request information and applications. If you know someone who teaches at a private school (or parents whose children attend one) talk with them to get a feel for the school and its policies.

Teaching Outside Your Home Town

In our survey, we found that most candidates look for teaching positions close to their colleges or close to where they grew up. While some candidates do find jobs in one of these two general areas, we suggest that you expand your area of job search for these reasons:

- ✓ Typically college towns have an oversupply of teacher-candidates.
- ✓ Unless you are a "fourth generation, been here forever, expect to be here forever" kind of person, you exclude some great opportunities by limiting your job search.

If you're willing to broaden your search area, there's a whole world of teaching opportunities out there waiting for you. You can apply for vacancies not only in other districts throughout your home state but in other states, as well. Also, there are thousands of overseas teaching opportunities, such as teaching for a private American school abroad, for a major U.S. corporation, or for the military. The Department of Defense, for example, operates 210 schools with a total enrollment of more than 100,000 American students.

Overseas positions almost always require that you be credentialed in one of the 50

> *Of the teacher candidates in our survey, 29 percent said they were willing to accept positions in private schools that may pay lower salaries.*

states and that you have done some graduate work or possess a graduate degree. Some also require fluency in a specific foreign language. Preference often is given to single teachers or to teaching couples with no children, because of a limited availability of housing.

If you are willing to consider teaching vacancies in other states, see the list of state departments of education and state offices of teacher credentialing in the appendix; the appendix also lists some great resources for overseas employment.

Make a Demonstration Video

Although rarely required by school districts as part of the screening process, demonstration videos are requested once in a while. Because of this, many colleges and universities include the preparation of a demo video as part of their teacher preparation courses. And a demo video is a necessity for anyone applying for a teaching position overseas or out of state, for which the interview is conducted by telephone. In this case, the demo video gives you a leg up on your competition because the hiring panel can see you "in person" and has a better sense of your personality and teaching style.

"Flexibility is the key. Limiting oneself to one district or one county can be problematic. An individual who can conduct a statewide or even a larger search greatly increases his chance of landing a great job."
—*Secondary music teacher in New Jersey*

As we researched this book, we found that 14 percent of those interviewed had prepared demonstration videos; and several reported having been asked by interview committees to leave a copy of their video for further review. Although such a request is not commonplace, it does happen—usually when the hiring panel is impressed with your performance at the interview and wants to see how you interact with a classroom full of students.

If you decide to put a demo video together, there are some things you should consider. The first is this: Play to your strengths. You know what you do best—use that in your video. It may be a particular science lesson you taught during your student teaching or a group activity in which you assume the role of facilitator. If you are doing your student teaching, your master teacher will probably be glad to work with you on this, and even do the taping for you. Most schools have a video camera available, so all you need is a high-quality tape.

You'll find that things you enjoy the most are ordinarily done best, so plan on having your favorite lessons put on your demo video. Here are some ideas to consider:

✓ Teach a lesson to the entire class, including all the steps of a well-planned lesson
✓ Teach a lesson to a smaller group
✓ Interact with a small group of students in cooperative groups or at an interest center
✓ Involve yourself in a physical education or game type of activity
✓ Direct a drama or musical event
✓ Work with another teacher in a team situation
✓ Work with the class or a small group on an art project
✓ Teach a song or musical activity
✓ Use manipulatives, especially as part of a science or math lesson
✓ Work with students in a community service setting

Your video should include segments of more than one lesson. The length of each should be long enough to get your message across, but not so long that it becomes boring.

Of the teacher-candidates in our survey, 14 percent said they had prepared demonstration videos as part of the job search.

Remember that you're in complete control of what a hiring panel will see, so give them your best by demonstrating all the energy, enthusiasm, and passion you can muster. Use your demonstration video as one more way to sell yourself.

Once you've completed your video, have copies made from the master. Label the copies in a clear, professional way and then put them to work for you. Let every school district know you have a demonstration video available, and always have one with you during an interview. Offer it to the committee, even if they don't ask for it. Once you've gone to the trouble and taken the time to create a video that showcases your talents, you ought to use it to your best advantage. It may be the "extra" that lands you the job.

Create a Teacher Portfolio

Teacher portfolios are rather new to the school job search scene, although many colleges and universities now require their students to create portfolios as part of their teacher credential programs. As this trend continues, it won't be long before these portfolios are expected at the interview table.

Before you begin filling your portfolio with everything in sight, however, let's consider its purpose. We can take a lesson here from corporate America, where portfolios have been around for a long time; in fact, they have been the professional's preferred mode of "show and tell" for years. It's a given, for example, that commercial artists bring along their portfolios when they interview with Madison Avenue ad agencies. Their portfolios contain carefully chosen samples of their work that speak for them at the interview table, demonstrating their talents. They know they have one chance, and one chance only, to shine—to make a great impression. No time to be too humble here.

The same principle applies to teachers: Your portfolio should show off your very best work. Gather up anything that demonstrates your talents, abilities, and accomplishments—anything that will put you in a special light with the hiring panel.

> *"Portfolios are nice, and here is a suggestion I found helpful: In the portfolio packets I assembled, I included a Recent Achievements Page—sort of a summary of things I have done. This also helped me summarize my most recent accomplishments and have them handy and fresh on my mind."*
> —Second-grade teacher in a parochial school in Massachusetts

If you have recently completed your student teaching, you probably have samples of your work, projects that took hours to prepare. If you haven't yet done your student teaching, however, begin thinking now about your portfolio as you begin your assignment.

Your portfolio begins with a sturdy folder, an accordion-style filing jacket, a presentation binder, or a heavy-duty portfolio with pockets (see your local office supply store for ideas). If you can afford it, you might even splurge on a leather-like portfolio, which gives a professional look.

You can fill your portfolio with anything you like—there are no rules—but here are some things you might want to include. Remember, the idea is to impress the interview panel with your skills and talents as a teacher, plus any transferable skills you have.

General Content

✓ Recent achievements page (a summary of what you've done lately)
✓ Resume
✓ Mission statement
✓ Professional letters of reference
✓ Letters from parents commending you for your work with their children
✓ Outstanding evaluations written by your university student teaching supervisor or your master teacher
✓ Copies of teaching certificates and certificates of participation in workshops or seminars
✓ Examples of the ways you recognize students' achievements (Student of the Month awards, etc.)

Classroom-Related Content

✓ Photos of you presenting a lesson to a class or working with a small group of students
✓ Photos of special activities (such as you taking your students on a field trip, directing a drama or musical presentation, participating as a school coach or yearbook adviser)
✓ Hands-on materials or manipulatives you have incorporated into a lesson

Note: Hands-on activities and manipulatives are hot trends in education, so it's important for you to work them into the interview somehow, especially if you have used them in math or science. This holds true for elementary and secondary.

✓ Samples of your students' work (art work, creative writing, etc.)
✓ A copy of your demo tape showing you in action (teaching a lesson, a song, or a game; working with a group of students, or one-on-one with a student)
✓ Copies of a specific, well-designed lesson plan

Community-Related Content

✓ Photos of you coaching a Little League team or working with children in the community in some way
✓ Photos of you working as a camp counselor, Sunday School teacher, or game director during a summer program
✓ Newspaper articles or photos that show you as a leader, a team player, an organizer, or a role model

Note: Try to include photos that are happy and upbeat; you want to convince the interview panel that you love kids, you love to teach, and you're having a lot of fun! In a word—SMILE!

We suggest that you mount everything possible in photo matting with dark, clear captions at the top of each mounting. For example:

"Teaching a Math Lesson Using Manipulatives"

"Serving as a Summer Camp Counselor"

It's a good idea, by the way, to have an inexpensive duplicate of your portfolio on hand, just in case the interview panel asks you to leave one with them.

We hope we've sold you on the concept of a teacher portfolio. Creating one is simple enough, and a well-organized portfolio is one more tool to make you stand out. Even if the interview speeds by and you never have a chance to share anything from your portfolio, at least you will have scored "style points." We know this is true because so many

"Bring something to the interview,

whether requested or not: a portfolio with

photos of previous classroom time,

a favorite lesson you designed or adapted,

samples of your lessons or projects.

This shows that you are prepared, even if the

opportunity does not arise to show it.

I've always noted when candidates have

something with them when they come in.

Just this alone tells me they want to

further present what they can do.

Attitude *and interest matter a* lot *to me!"*

—*Principal of a rural middle school in Virginia.*

of the administrators we interviewed said they were impressed when a teacher-candidate brought a portfolio to the interview. It shows them you have that something extra, something your competition may not have.

2

Making the Paper Cut

You won't be hired without an interview, and you won't be interviewed unless you make the paper cut. The paper cut is a school district's initial screening process that determines whether you will be asked to interview or not. Because it's so important for you to make this cut, it's crucial that you understand the concept.

To begin with, the paper we're referring to here includes all the pieces of paper submitted to a school district in your pursuit of a teaching position. Depending on the district's requirements, these may include a resume, letters of reference, an application, a cover letter, copies of your college transcripts, or information forwarded from your college career placement file.

Every school district has its own paper screening philosophy. Here are some of the most common.

Screening Procedures

Many larger school districts use a process whereby one elementary and one secondary principal are designated to screen applicants' papers at their respective grade levels. During this initial screening, the better papers are placed in an active file (or applicant pool) for a certain period of time, usually one school year. This applicant pool is used as a resource when a teaching vacancy occurs or when there is a need to hire a long-term substitute.

The poorer papers are either discarded or placed in an inactive file, where they are seldom (or never) seen again. This inactive file is discarded at the end of each school year.

When a specific teaching vacancy occurs, it is advertised. Any applications or resumes received as a result are sent to the site administrator (usually the principal) for screening, along with those in the active file. The top five or ten applicants are then chosen by the site administrator.

Depending on the school district's philosophy, these applications may be referred to an interview team for further screening before interviews are scheduled, or the site administrator may decide which of the candidates will be scheduled. Shared decision making is a popular philosophy these days, especially among the larger school districts, although some districts place great emphasis on giving the school's principal sole decision-making power.

An interview team, by the way, usually consists of the site administrator, teachers, parents, and school board members or community residents. An interview may be conducted by an interview team (also known as an interview committee or a hiring panel) or solely by the site administrator.

Many large school districts have well-staffed personnel departments who do the initial screening of all applicants, whether they are applying for current or future vacancies. The personnel director and his or her staff make the first paper cut, placing the top applicants for each type of vacancy in active files that are delivered to the principals at schools where specific vacancies exist. The principals choose the top candidates from these prescreened files to be scheduled for interviews with a hiring panel or with the principal him- or herself.

Smaller school districts often bypass these initial screenings and refer all applicants' files directly to the principal at the school where an opening exists. This administrator does all the work: screens the files, makes the paper cut, and schedules the top candidates for interviews.

Whatever the district's philosophy, however, you won't be scheduled for an interview unless your file makes it past the initial screening process—and our goal is to help you do just that.

Teacher-Specific Resumes

There are dozens of books available at your library or local book store on the subject of resume writing, but it could take a week or more to glean the *specific* information you need to a prepare a teacher resume. Resume requirements differ greatly from profession to profession, so what we've included in this chapter are the specifics that pertain to the field of education. We also have included model resumes in various formats.

Outstanding Resumes

You may never have needed a resume until now, and the very thought of writing one may seem overwhelming. Your fears are understandable, but we guarantee you'll feel much better about the whole thing once you've read through this section. We've tried to simplify the process of resume writing by giving you some clear, concise direction in a question-answer format. Fortunately, a teacher's resume is less complex than those required in some other professions.

What Is a Resume?

A resume is a concise, easy-to-read history of your life that includes personal data, job objective, educational background, employment history, community service, work skills, and accomplishments. There are three basic resume styles: *chronological, functional,* and *combination.* A resume (along with the application and letters of reference) is the tool most district personnel use to screen teacher candidates before scheduling interviews.

Why Is a Resume Important?

A resume is one of the most important tools you will use in your job search. It is a representation of yourself—an indication of who you are. An outstanding, flawless resume can eventually land you an interview; likewise, a poorly written, sloppy resume will kill your chances. An effective resume should include the information most likely to impress the particular school or district to which you are applying. If you impress the screeners with your resume, as well as your application and letters of reference, they will schedule you for an interview; you will have made the paper cut. Unless you survive this cut, or initial screening process, you will never make it to the interview table.

How Long Should a Resume Be?

If you are a recent college graduate with limited work experience, a one-page resume is ideal. If you have extensive work experience, however, a page and a half to two pages should be the limit. If your resume is longer than one page, however, you're taking the risk that only the first page will be read, especially if the personnel office is swamped with applicants.

What's the Difference Between Chronological, Functional, and Combination Resumes?

1. **Chronological Resumes** list your employment experience in reverse chronological order, starting with your most recent position and working backward in time.

Advantages: Easy to write, easy to read, and widely accepted by school district personnel.

Disadvantages: Not a good choice if you have little or no work history; if you have been a job hopper or are changing careers; or if there have been long lapses between employment.

2. **Functional Resumes**, also known as **Skills Resumes**, emphasize your skills, strengths, and accomplishments.

    Advantages: Popular choice for recent college graduates; provides a practical format for selling yourself by accentuating your strengths and transferable skills.

    Disadvantages: Difficult to organize and to read unless very well-formatted.

3. **Combination Resumes**, also known as **Creative Resumes**, combine elements of chronological and functional resumes. These are the most creative and adaptable types of resumes and are the favorite choice of many teacher applicants.

    Advantages: Uses the best ideas from both styles: teaching experience, related experience, activities and distinctions, interests, skills, and educational background; allows for a great deal of creativity.

    Disadvantages: More time-consuming to organize and difficult to read unless formatted very carefully.

What Do You Mean by "Formatting?"

Formatting is the way the information is laid out on the page. There are two basic styles of formatting:

1. **Block Style** has a clean, sharp appearance because all the headings begin at the left margin. The information under each heading is indented about an inch

and a half, giving it an "airy" look with a lot of white space.

2. **Centered Style** uses full margins and wider lines. This is an excellent choice if you have a great deal of information to include on a one-page resume. It is not as crisp-looking as the block style and is more difficult to read.

> *"What impresses me most about a candidate's resume and application is the professional presentation and the experiences outside of education that can be of benefit in dealing with kids. Also, brag a little. As they say, if you can do it, it's not bragging. Besides, you only have a few pieces of paper to prove you should be interviewed!"*
>
> —*Science chair, mentor teacher, and member of interview committee for a rural district in Northern California*

What Is a Customized Resume?

A customized resume is one that is targeted toward a specific teaching vacancy.

For example, if you are applying for a position as a high school social studies teacher with adjunct duties as cheerleading adviser, you would want to include your high school and college cheerleading experiences; the fact that your cheerleading team at U.C.L.A. won first place in the Western Division finals; and your stints teaching at a summer high school cheerleading camp.

If you're applying for an overseas position teaching German to American students in Munich, you would devote a large chunk of space to your mastery of the German language; the summer you lived with a German family in Bremen; and your knowledge of the German culture.

If you're applying for a position as a high school English and drama teacher who will be required to direct two dramatic productions each year, you'll want to emphasize your Little Theater work; your summer experience directing a traveling production of *Our Town*; and the dramas you put together for your church youth program.

Obviously, a customized resume is a smart way to market yourself when you have transferable skills or experiences that match the special requirements listed in a job description.

What Are the Basic Rules of Resume Writing?

- ✓ Use 8 1/2" by 11" white or off-white paper, 20-pound bond or better
- ✓ Never use the pronoun "I"
- ✓ Make all headings uniform
- ✓ Vary the font size between 10 and 12 points, except for your name, which may be in 14- to 24-point type
- ✓ Don't make anything larger than your name
- ✓ If the resume has two or more pages, number each page and include your name
- ✓ Never use a staple or paper clip
- ✓ Never print on both sides of the paper
- ✓ Don't get too cute with novelty graphics, gothic fonts, shadowed letters, or fancy borders; this is not an art project
- ✓ Prepare the resume on a typewriter or word processor; the latter is preferable because it offers various font sizes and the ability to update or customize the resume on short notice
- ✓ If the resume is computer-generated, use a laser quality printer, if possible

How Long Does It Take to Write a Resume?

A simple chronological resume may take as little as two hours, but a functional or combination resume will take from five to fifteen hours. You don't sit down over a cup of coffee and write your resume like you would a personal letter. It takes a great deal of thought, information gathering, creative writing, and editing. Many resume writing experts even suggest that you work on it an hour or so at a time—then come back to it the next day. (You can see why professional resume writers don't come cheap.)

What Is an Unacceptable Resume?

A resume with any of these qualities:

✓ Handwritten
✓ Typos or misspelled words
✓ Long sentences that ramble on and on
✓ Lack of organization
✓ Use of the pronoun "I"
✓ A "crowded" look with little white space
✓ Poor print quality
✓ Handwritten corrections
✓ A shopworn look (bent corners, creases, smudges, or stains)

A member of an interview committee for a suburban district in Michigan was asked what impressed him most about a resume or application, and this was his response: "Brevity—ability to get to the point."

What Makes a Resume Outstanding?

According to our research, these are the qualities school district personnel directors hope to see:

✓ Brief and concise
✓ Easy to read
✓ No more than three to five headings
✓ Tasteful use of font sizes, italics, boldface print, underlining, and capital letters
✓ Uniform margins, preferably no smaller than an inch
✓ A crisp, clean, professional look
✓ Power verbs
✓ No amateurish gimmicks
✓ Skills, talents, and abilities that are transferable to the classroom

✓ **No typos**
✓ **No misspelled words**

We've emphasized these last two qualities because we heard them over and over again during our research, and we can't stress them enough! The personnel people who do the initial screening of applications and resumes expect perfection; they often feel that teachers, above all, should be able to spell and avoid typographical errors. So be warned: There is practically no room for error here.

Recently, a company called Office Team surveyed executives of companies nationwide and asked how they felt about these same resume flaws. The results of the survey show that standards in the business world are not very different than standards in the educational arena:

✓ The general attitude is "Two strikes and you're out," meaning that any combination of two typos or misspelled words disqualifies the candidate from further consideration.

✓ Nearly 45 percent of the executives polled said it only takes *one* of these errors to eliminate the candidate from the running!

Obviously, it's imperative that you avoid these errors, and this is what we recommend to ensure a flawless resume:

✓ Run a "spell check," if possible.

✓ Use a dictionary to look up the spelling of *any* word in doubt.

✓ Give copies of your resume to several peers to review and edit.

✓ Read your resume backwards, beginning with the last word at the bottom of the page and ending at the top. This is a clever trick that catches typos and misspelled words often missed when reading normally, because it forces you to see only one word at a time. (Try finding the mistake in this sentence by reading it backwords and you'll see what we mean.)

What Are "Power" Verbs?

Power verbs are what bring a resume to life. A power verb reveals an impressive ability or character trait in a single word. Use them liberally throughout your resume. Here are some examples:

✓ Achieved
✓ Administered
✓ Attained
✓ Chaired
✓ Coached
✓ Communicated
✓ Completed
✓ Conducted
✓ Coordinated
✓ Created
✓ Delegated
✓ Demonstrated
✓ Developed
✓ Devised
✓ Directed
✓ Drafted
✓ Encouraged
✓ Established
✓ Evaluated
✓ Expedited
✓ Facilitated
✓ Formulated
✓ Founded
✓ Guided
✓ Helped
✓ Implemented
✓ Improved
✓ Influenced
✓ Initiated
✓ Installed
✓ Instructed
✓ Interacted
✓ Interviewed
✓ Introduced

✓ Judged
✓ Led
✓ Maintained
✓ Managed
✓ Molded
✓ Motivated
✓ Negotiated
✓ Operated
✓ Organized
✓ Originated
✓ Perfected
✓ Performed
✓ Persuaded
✓ Planned
✓ Prepared
✓ Presented
✓ Presided
✓ Produced
✓ Promoted
✓ Proposed
✓ Recommended
✓ Researched
✓ Resolved
✓ Scheduled
✓ Selected
✓ Solved
✓ Supervised
✓ Taught
✓ Tested
✓ Trained
✓ Troubleshot
✓ Updated
✓ Utilized
✓ Wrote

Should I List My References on My Resume?

The consensus of opinion is that you should not. There are several reasons for this:

- ✓ You don't want to unnecessarily subject your references to constant telephone calls.
- ✓ It takes up too much valuable space.
- ✓ Employers already know you have a list of references and will request a copy if they are seriously interested in you.

By the way, the jury seems to be out on whether or not to include this phrase at the bottom of your resume:

References available upon request.

Many feel it is a waste of space because employers already know this.

Note: At present in California thousands of new teachers are being hired at the primary level, much of it "on the spot" hiring. This is due to a movement to reduce classroom size to 20 students in grades K-3. One personnel director shared with us that because of this downsizing, his district personnel people were concurrently screening candidates in one room, interviewing in another, and actually hiring in yet another. This may not be atypical around the state. So, if you should find yourself caught up in a hiring frenzy like this, it would probably be wise to include your references on your resume.

Sample Resumes

Now that you have a handle on the basics, here are nine well-written samples that demonstrate these basics in a variety of styles. Choose the one that comes closest to your qualifications, interests, specializations, and experiences, then build from there, capitalizing on your own strengths and abilities.

Resume #1

KAREN McCRAE
2117 Bennington Way • Taylorville, IL 60005 • (703) 555-1908

OBJECTIVE
> **Teacher: High School History and French**
> Coach: High School Girl's Basketball

EDUCATION
> **Lincoln University**, Arlington Heights, Illinois
> B.A. Degree - June, 1998
> > **Major:** History   **Minor:** French
>
> **Taylorville Community College**, Taylorville, Illinois
> > A.A. Degree - June, 1995
> > **Major:** History

STUDENT TEACHING
> **Craymont High School, 142 Smith Valley Rd., Craymont, IL   1/98-6/98**

Responsibilities:
- Taught sophomore U. S. History class for eight weeks
- Taught junior World History class for eight weeks
- Worked individually with at-risk students in History
- Assisted students with school history periodical, <u>Saga</u>
- Assisted students with school historical drama production
- Acted as assistant coach for girls varsity basketball team
- Worked with students in computer historical research program, "How, When, Where, Why"

Treyton High School, Newport, IL   9/97-12/97

Responsibilities:
- Observed and assisted in various History classes
- Assisted in French I and French 11 classes
- Worked in French language lab with individual students
- Assistant coach for girls J. V. volleyball team

RELATED ACTIVITIES
- Volunteer tutor - Treyton High School library computer center
- Coach/referee - Newport Community Recreation Center
- Coached at Edwards Girls Basketball Camp, summer '95
- Served as chaperone for high school tour of France, '96
- Toured major European countries 6/97 - 8/97
- Member State Historical Society, past President, local chapter
- Advisor to French Club at Treyton High School

CREDENTIALS/REFERENCES
> College Placement Office, Lincoln University,
> 123 Newberry Street, Arlington Heights, IL 60001
> Telephone (703) 555-2000

Resume #2

JOHN R. MOST

1743 Washington Blvd. • Village Park, MI 49022 • (617) 555-0423

TEACHING OBJECTIVE
  Bilingual Second Grade Teacher

STRENGTHS/ABILITIES
  • Works well with at-risk students
  • Extensive course work in early childhood education
  • Taught multicultural classes
  • Speaks Spanish fluently

TEACHING EXPERIENCE
  Julian Elementary School, Essex, MI   Fall Semester '97

  • Student teacher, first/second grade bilingual class
  • Worked with small group of underachieving math students
  • Conducted fifteen parent-teacher conferences
  • Designed and executed lessons in English/Spanish
  • Assumed all classroom teaching responsibilities for four weeks

CLASSROOM EXPERIENCE
  • Applegate Elementary School, York, IN   Spring '97
      Observation/cadet teaching - third grade
  • Fremont Elementary School, York IN   Spring '97
      Math tutor - third grade
  • Julian Elementary School, Your Town, IN   Spring '97
      Participated in individual reading program - third grade

COLLEGE ACTIVITIES
  • Local NEA Chapter - member two years
  • Big Brothers Club - member three years, President '97
  • Student Body Treasurer '96-'97
  • Track team - four years

COMMUNITY SERVICE
  • Student representative to city council
  • Co-chair college/city "We Love Our City Day"
  • Assistant coach - Little League baseball, two years

EDUCATIONAL BACKGROUND
  Eaton Falls State Teacher's College, Essex, MI
  Bachelor of Arts Degree June, 1998
    Major: Elementary Education; Minor: English

CREDENTIALS/REFERENCES
  College Placement Office, 121 Mione Way, Essex, MI 49018
  Telephone (617) 555-2222, FAX (617) 555-2226

Resume #3

TRACY E. RICHARDSON
900 Arrowhead Dr. • Telephone: (515) 555-3446 • Des Moines, IA 50309

OBJECTIVE: A position as a secondary school Social Studies teacher.

EDUCATION: *Master of Arts* in *Teaching,* October, 1997
Quinnipiac College, Hamden, CT
Dean's List, Recipient of merit-based fellowship award

Bachelor of Science, May, 1991
University of Wisconsin, Madison, WI
Dean's List, College of Letters and Science Honors Program participant

CERTIFICATION: *Wisconsin Social Studies Teaching Licenses:* Broad Field (701), History (725), Psychology (740), and Sociology (745).

PROFESSIONAL EXPERIENCE:

Sept., 1996 - *Substitute Teacher.* Fairfield Public Schools. Fairfield, CT
Jan., 1997   Taught all ability levels and subject areas, grades six through twelve.

Jan., 1995 - *Student Teacher.* Haddam-Killingworth Middle School. Higganum, CT
April, 1996   Taught eighth grade Social Studies classes. Curriculum focused on U.S. History and included the use of supplementary source materials and activities.

Sept., 1986 - *Senior Product Marketing Specialist.* Data Switch Corporation. Shelton, CT
May, 1989   Developed and presented product training courses and specialized application seminars. Managed the growth of a $20 million product line.

RELATED EXPERIENCE:

Sept., 1997 - *Tutor.* School Volunteer Association of Bridgeport, Inc. Bridgeport, CT
Dec., 1997   Tutored students in basic and remedial reading, math, and computer skills in classroom settings.

Sept., 1996 - *Advisor.* Department of Youth Services. Fairfield, CT
Jan., 1997   Training coordinator for student and adult volunteers in Safe Rides program.

Nov., 1995 - *Assistant Women's Basketball Coach.* Notre Dame High School. Fairfield, CT
Mar., 1997   Provided instruction in basketball skills and strategies for varsity and jr. varsity teams.

Jan., 1989 - *Research Assistant.* University of Wisconsin, Madison, WI
May, 1990   Scheduled and conducted experiments, assisted in planning research projects, and analyzed data under the direction of Sociology and Psychology professors.

Sept., 1986 - *Undergraduate Tutor.* University of Wisconsin, Madison, WI
May, 1987   Tutored introductory level courses. Evaluated and placed students seeking academic assistance.

Summer, *Camp Counselor.* Red Pine Camp, Woodruff, WI
1986   Taught basketball and archery. Coordinated daily activities for a group of sixth graders.

Sept., 1980 - *Youth Counselor.* Local youth group. Madison, WI
Aug., 1984   Supervised recreational activities of seventh and eighth grade students.

SPECIAL SKILLS: *Personal Computer Expertise.* Extensive experience with IBM compatible and Apple Macintosh systems, including education, word processing, spreadsheet, database, and graphics applications.

American Red Cross Training. Certified in CPR and Basic First Aid.

MEMBERSHIPS: National Council for the Social Studies, Wisconsin Council for the Social Studies, University of Wisconsin Alumni Association

Resume #4

Allyson Corley

116 Parmac Road / Ellis, WI 32770 / (604) 555-9852

Objective
I seek a position teaching English at the secondary level. I would be interested in traditional, alternative or experimental programs, full or part-time positions. I am willing to be involved with student assistance programs, class and club sponsorship and publications advising.

Experience
Alternative School Teacher *North Adams Community Schools COPE Program, Decatur, IN. (209) 555-1112. August 1992 to May 1994. Coordinator: Helen Matthews.* Taught English and Social Studies to court-appointed middle school students. As part of a team, responsible for assisting students not only with their academic goals but also with the emotional and behavioral problems which kept them from being successful at the regular middle school. Also taught English to students at ACCES alternative high school during the 1993-94 school year.

English Teacher/Publications Adviser *Elkhart High School, Elkhart, IL. (871) 555-1610. August 1988 to November 1991. Principal: Hazel Bringan.* Taught Advanced Composition, American Literature, Journalism. Advised yearbook staff 3 1/4 years, newspaper staff 2-1/4 years.

Summer School English Teacher *Mayflower School District, 1988 Senior High Summer School Program, Mayflower, MI. (581) 555-2002. June to July 1988. Principal: Tom Saunders.* Taught two sections of 9th grade English.

English Education Student Teacher *Mayflower High School, Mayflower, MI. (581) 555-6672. August to December 1987. Supervising Teacher: Jeffrey Tompkins.* Taught two sections of 11th grade English and two sections of Writing I.

Education
Bachelor of Arts degree, **English Education,** Michigan State University, East Lansing, 1988. Certification: Indiana Teacher's License in English, grades 5-12; Michigan Provisional Certificate, All Subjects, 7-8, Social Studies and English, 9-12; currently in process of obtaining certification in Ohio.

Graduate courses (22 credits) in Counseling, Literature, Yearbook and Newspaper Advising. *Staff development* through Concord Community Schools: Student Assistance Program (including formal intervention training), Management Systems Training I & H, Teacher Expectations-Student Achievement, Intro. to Cooperative Learning. *Conferences:* Indiana Department of Education At-Risk Conference, February 1993; Healthy Adolescence, May 1993; Working with Difficult Students, October 1993.

Achievements
- Helped create COPE program, from establishing objectives to implementing daily routine
- Restructured journalism offerings at Concord High School
- Initiated progressive changes in high school newspaper organization and format
- Played in women's soccer Governor's Cup championships, 1989, 1990, 1991
- Graduated from Michigan State with high honors, Phi Beta Kappa
- Child care volunteer for YWCA Women 's Shelter Rural Outreach Program

References available upon request.

Resume #5

Gloria Benson

2420 Hinton Avenue · Dallas, Texas 37120 · (214) 555-0009

OBJECTIVE

Teacher: EARLY CHILDHOOD EDUCATION

EDUCATION

University of Texas, Austin, Texas
B.A. Degree - June, 1996
Major: Early Childhood Education
Area of Specialization: English Literature

COURSE HIGHLIGHTS

- Early Childhood Teaching
- Educational Psychology
- Child Development
- Children's Literature

STUDENT TEACHING EXPERIENCE

Sunnybrooke Farm Day School, Austin, Texas, 10/95 - 12/95

Responsibilities:
- Taught beginning math concepts to small cluster groups
- Designed plans for cooperative group activities
- Created instructional and seasonal bulletin boards
- Constructed interest centers for Reading and Math
- Planned ESL lessons for language minority children
- Maintained students' progress reports
- Participated in parent/teacher conferences

Lyndon B. Johnson School, Austin, Texas, third grade, 1/96 - 3/96

Responsibilities:
- Taught integrated units on: Poetry; American Indians; Rocks and Minerals
- Created interest centers for Reading, Math Manipulatives; Creative Writing
- Taught reading to advanced level reading group
- Maintained progress charts and records for all students
- Attended "Student Study Team" meetings for Learning Disability Children

RELATED ACTIVITIES

- Reading clinic volunteer, University of Texas Department of Education, Summer Program, 1995
- Organized Literature Appreciation program at Alamand Community Center
- Member, Klassics for Kids literature program, Austin, Texas

REFERENCES

College Placement Center, University of Texas, Austin, Texas 37098
(817) 753-2099; FAX (817) 753-2033

Resume #6

BETH R. ALEXANDER

Current Address:	Permanent Address:
2200 Alder Way	158 N. Potter
Santa Ana, CA 92701	Berkeley, CA 94705
(714) 555-3121	(510) 555-6998

OBJECTIVE A teaching position in Kindergarten - Twelfth grade.

EDUCATION **RADFORD UNIVERSITY** Radford, VA
Bachelor of Science May 1996, Physical Education,
Major GPA: 3.8, Overall GPA: 3.6 Dean's List for 4 semesters

ACTIVITIES
- **Physical Education Majors Club-** Treasurer; Junior Representative; Assisted with Saturday Morning Program teaching 75 kids ages 5-12 soccer, gymnastics, and swimming
- **Radford University Tour Guide-** Showed prospective students and families around the campus and answered their questions; Assisted in giving interviews to Tour Guide applicants
- **Student Mentor** for Freshman
- **Baptist Student Union-** President; Missions Director; Family Group Leader; Planned several fundraising events, raising over $2,000
- **Intramurals** Participant (Basketball, Softball, and Volleyball)
- **Virginia Association for Health, Physical Education, Recreation, and Dance Member** Elected Student Representative ('94-96); Attended and Voted in State Board Meetings

RELATED EXPERIENCE *Radford High School* Radford, VA
EIGHTH GRADE GIRL'S BASKETBALL CO-HEAD COACH 7/95-9/96
- Ran and prepared practice schedules
- Made decisions during games regarding 20 players and plays
- Responsible for equipment, trainer duties, and statistics

ASSISTANT INDOOR TRACK COACH 11/94-2/95
- Established workouts for field event participants and sprinters
- Coached 16 high school athletes

VARSITY GIRL'S BASKETBALL ASSISTANT COACH 3/94-10/94
- Recorded statistical information
- Assisted with game preparation, decision making, and the organization of practice
- Worked and coached 19 athletes

Virginia Baptist General Board Richmond, VA
SPORTS DAY CAMP INSTRUCTOR 5/94-7/94

- Conducted sports day camps for elementary age children varying from 15-60 children
- Prepared games and activities to incorporate fundamental skills

Radford High School Radford, VA
ASSISTANT TRACK COACH 3/94-5/94 3/93-5/93 3/92-5/92

- Instructed athletes with individual skills and events
- Assisted with daily workouts for practice
- Helped organize All American Relays with other coaches

Radford High School Radford, VA
JUNIOR VARSITY AND VARSITY CHEERLEADING COACH 11/94-2/95

- Established rules and logistics
- Supervised 15 girls during practice and games

EMPLOYMENT *Good Shepard Baptist Church* Christiansburg, VA
EXPERIENCE **SUMMER YOUTH DIRECTOR** 6/96-7/96

- Planned activities for youth ages 12 and up
- Led studies, childrens church, and children sermons
- Met with the Youth Committee monthly to finalize plans

Chic-fil-a Spotsylvania, VA
CASHIER 4/91-10/93

- Communication with management, employment, and customers
- Helped train new employees on cash register

Indian Acres Club of Thornburg Thornburg, VA
RECREATION ASSISTANT 3/93-9/93

- Assisted with planning for holiday events and tournaments
- Checked equipment in and out

Montgomery Ward Spotsylvania, VA
CASHIER 4/92-8/93

- Maintained a clean Men's department
- Communication with others
- Responsible for register transactions

CONFERENCES Attended VAHPERD State Conference (Nov 94); presided over 3 seminars

Attended VAHPERD Student Leadership Conference (Mar 95)

Attended VAHPERD State Conference (Nov 95); planned and led student activities and presentations

AVAILABILITY May 1996

REFERENCES Available upon request

Resume #7

Patricia Winston
321 Oakdale Rd. #303 | Merced, AZ 13318 | Home Phone: (707) 555-1881

EDUCATION

Butte Community College	GE Requirements
ASU, Merced	Graduated: December 1994
BA: Liberal Studies	
ASU, Merced Graduate School	1/95 - 12/95
Multiple Subject Credential	

PROFESSIONAL EXPERIENCE

Preschool Teacher Aide 1/96-Present
> Waldorf based learning approach; taught using hands-on activities and provided opportunities to develop social skills and self-esteem.
> Country Creek Preschool, 945 Pine Ave., Merced, AZ 13318. (707) 555-2708

K-2 Student Teacher　　　　　　　　　Fall 1995
> Open Structure Classroom. All subjects with special responsibilities in a whole language literacy program and hands-on mathematics
> Garrow Elementary, Merced Unified School District, Merced, AZ 13318

5th Grade Student Teacher　　　　　　Spring 1995
> Self-contained GATE class; all subjects with a focus on language arts.
> Marigold Elementary, Merced Unified School District, Merced, AZ 13318

Classroom Aide　　　　　　　　　　　Fall 1994
> Approx. 8 1 hr sessions with 3rd and 4th grade classes to instruct Physical Education.
> Supervisor: Prof. John Henderson, ASU. (707) 555-6181
> Rosedale Elementary Merced Unified School District, Merced; AZ 13318

English tutor for ESL student.　　　　Fall 1994
> 1 hr/week. Special Focus on increasing vocabulary and improving writing skills

Classroom Aide　　　　　　　　　　　Spring 1994
> 34hrs. Aided in a 1/2 classroom, worked with reading and math groups.
> Marigold Elementary, Merced Unified School District, Merced, AZ 13318

Classroom Aide　　　　　　　　　　　9/87-6/98
> 1 hr/week. Worked with mild and severely disabled children in a special day class.
> Duties included teaching living skills, writing, math and reading.
> Harmon School, Tucson, AZ

WORK EXPERIENCE

The Gathering Place　　　　8/95-Present
Title: Program Aide, working with disabled adults.　　(707) 555-3228

The Victorian Guest Home　　　　6/95-8/95
Title: Activity Leader, worked with the elderly　　(707) 555-8971

Holiday Inn, Merced　　　7/89-3-95
Title: Assistant Executive Housekeeper　　(707) 555-0008

SPECIAL INTEREST/ACTIVITIES

Enjoy: hiking, cooking, reading, learning sign language and learning to play the piano.

Member of SCTA and Kappa Delta Pi

REFERENCES are available at your request from the Career Placement Office, Arizona State University, Merced, AZ 13318 (707) 555-3351

Resume #8

Dena Riley

1815 Cedar Reedley, CA 95660 — (906)555-8530

Objective	To be an elementary school teacher who will inspire children to learn and to become life long learners.
Highlights of Qualifications	• Eight years experience working with children ages two to ten • Strong practical and theoretical foundation in Early Childhood Education
Professional Experience	**Bilingual Kindergarten, Student Teaching** (Nov. 1995-Feb. 1996) Torrance Elementary, Hamilton Union Elementary School District: Torrance, California
	First/Second Grade, (Aug. 1995-Nov. 1995) **Open Classroom, Student Teaching** Eldridge School, Branson Unified School District: Branson, California
	Child Care Provider (July 1993-July 1995) Stepping Stones Children's Center, Branson, California
	Child Care Provider (July 1988-Dec. 1992) Story Book Nursery School, Reedley, California
Curriculum	• Implemented state framework based curriculum • Integrated thematic units • Planned and taught literature-based units • Instructed MathLand, Math Their Way and Math Excursions • Activities in FOSS Science and Wonderworks Science • Writer's Workshop • Implemented Here's Looking at You 2000
Methodology	• Direct Instructional Model • Cooperative Group Learning • Hands On Activities • Literature based reading program • Whole language lessons/activities • E.S.L. • S.D.A.I.E.

Education	**CLAD** Credential - 1996
	Professional Clear
	Multiple Subject Credential
	    Fresno State University, 1996
	        Bachelor of Arts - Psychology: Fresno State University, 1993
	        Sixty-nine units completed: Butte Community College, 1988

Professional Growth	California Kindergarten Conference: San Francisco State University, 1966 Strength Through Diversity Seminar: Fresno State University, 1996 Parent Effectiveness Training, 1993 Internship - Children's Education Fund, 1991
References	References are available upon request from the Career Planning and Placement Office, Fresno State University, Fresno, CA 95311. (209) 555-4030

Resume #9

MARK J. THOMAS
811 Newton Avenue
Boulder, Colorado 80301
(200) 555-1001

EDUCATION
May 1993
University of Colorado, Boulder, Colorado
Bachelor of Arts Degree with
Multiple Subject Teaching Credential
Minor in English

PROFESSIONAL EXPERIENCE

9/93-7/97   4th Grade, Rockyview Elementary School,
Superior Unified School District, Superior, CO

- Taught all subjects in a self-contained classroom
- Designed integrated thematic units, hands-on math learning center; and science and math interest centers
- Tutored one-on-one with four learning disabled students

1/93-5/92   5th grade student teacher, Chandler Middle School,
Boulder Valley, Colorado

- Developed thematic units
- Taught one ESL class
- Adapted and taught poetry unit
- Participated in grade level curriculum study
- Implemented "Reading for Pleasure" remedial reading program

6/92-9/92   Private tutor

- Worked one-on-one with learning disabled student
- Developed and taught customized lessons in math and reading

RELATED EXPERIENCE

- Game director for AWANA children's clubs
- Coach boys' Pop Warner football
- Wrote and directed children's Christmas musical

References available upon request.

Note: Keep a record of every resume you send out or hand deliver, and be especially careful to save a copy of any resume that has been customized for a specific job vacancy.

If you've read resumes 1 through 9 and still feel unsure about writing your own, contact your college career placement office. There you will find professionals trained to help you.

Winning Applications

After all the work you've done up to this point—assessing your strengths and weaknesses, preparing your mission statement, writing your resume—the application itself might seem like a piece of cake. Unfortunately, it is not.

> *"Take your application seriously—it's an initial representation of yourself."*
>
> —Secondary English teacher who has served on interview committees in Ohio

Your application, like your resume, is a representation of you—serious stuff! If a district's personnel office receives more than 100 applications for a teaching vacancy (which is common in many school districts), the staff has only so much time to scan each one in the stack. These people are sharp, however: Their eyes are trained, and they are able to rule out many applicants after only a quick glance at the applications. They do this based not only on the content of the applications but on how neatly and carefully they were prepared. Therefore, you want your application to make the best impression possible, so it will work for you instead of against you.

Here's how to make yours a winning application.

Content

The first step is to gather up all the information you will need to fill out the application:

- ✓ **Educational background,** with dates attended and graduated
- ✓ **Professional experience,** with dates and addresses
- ✓ **Other work experience,** with dates, addresses, and reasons for leaving
- ✓ **Teaching credentials** held and their expiration dates
- ✓ **Professional references,** including addresses and telephone numbers
- ✓ **Personal information,** including Social Security Number
- ✓ **Honors, awards, and fellowships** you have received
- ✓ **Special skills** or related experiences

As you gather this information, enter it on an actual application form; that way, you'll have everything together in one place when you need it. Following is a sample application you can use for this purpose.

LAKETOWN HIGH SCHOOL
Laketown, Illinois
CERTIFICATED APPLICATION
Personnel Services: (501) 555-8000
FAX: (501) 555-8004
AN EQUAL OPPORTUNITY EMPLOYER

Regular _____
Substitute _____
Home Teaching _____

FOR PERSONNEL OFFICE USE
Entry Date _____
By _____

PERSONAL:

_____ Social Security No. _____
Last Name   First Name   M.I.

Present
Address _____ Phone ( ) _____
                         (Street)

_____
(City and State)   (Zip)
Permanent
Address _____ Phone ( ) _____
                         (Street)

_____
(City and State)   (Zip)

POSITION DESIRED:

Level Preference: List subject and/or grade level of preference:

____ ELEMENTARY (K-5)   _____

____ MIDDLE (6-8)   _____

____ HIGH SCHOOL (9-12)   _____

____ OTHER   _____

Please list other languages you speak: _____

ILLINOIS CREDENTIAL INFORMATION:

Expiration
Date

Illinois Credentials now held   _____   _____

                                 _____   _____

If no Illinois credential now, have you applied for one? **YES** ____ **NO** ____

What type? _____ When? _____

Do you hold an out-of-state credential?

YES ___ **NO** ___ What type? _____ State _____

FOR PERSONNEL OFFICE USE

EDUCATION AND PROFESSIONAL TRAINING: (College or University only)

Name and Location of Institution Attended	Dates Attended From To	Major(s)	Minor	Graduation Date – Degrees

TEACHING AND/OR ADMINISTRATIVE EXPERIENCE:

Total years of full-time, paid teaching experience: _____ Total years of administrative and/or supervisory experience:_____ LIST ALL EXPERIENCE BY POSITIONS IN CHRONOLOGICAL ORDER. ADMINISTRATORS NEED NOT LIST STUDENT TEACHING. FOR TEACHER APPLICANTS, LIST STUDENT TEACHING FIRST. DO NOT COUNT STUDENT TEACHING IN TOTAL YEARS TAUGHT.

Dates	Location (City/State)	Name/Level of School	Grade or Subjects Taught	Salary
				Student Teaching

Be positive and creative as you enter the information on the application form. For example, when entering previous job titles, responsibilities, and reasons for leaving, use the most glowing terms possible without compromising the truth. You should also use as many power verbs as possible (see the list earlier in this chapter).

Say, for example, you worked one summer emptying trash and wet-mopping the halls of an office building after closing time each business day. You might say: "Maintained and secured building." (Surely, you locked up when you left, didn't you?) The words "maintained" and "secured" are power verbs.

Another good idea is to customize your application in much the same way as you would a resume, by including any skills, training, awards, work experiences, or activities that match the job vacancy you want to fill. This is a way to "load" the application in your favor so that you appear more qualified than other applicants.

As you indulge in this "creative writing," always choose your words carefully, and never use more words than necessary—they clutter up the page.

If you have a gimmicky, cute message on your answering machine, replace it with something more professional, like this: "You have reached 555-9085. Please leave a message at the beep."

Preparation

It's always best to type an application, using a fresh ribbon and a smaller-size font. If you are visiting various schools and personnel offices as part of your school survey and are handed an application to fill out, take it home with you rather than filling it out on the spot. That way, you'll be able to use a typewriter, correct any errors with correction fluid or correction tape, and proofread it carefully before actually submitting it. As a precaution, we suggest making a copy of the application, filling the copy out first as a rough draft, then recopying your information onto the original form.

However, if time is of the essence and it is imperative that you complete the application then and there, be sure to print, using an erasable dark black pen. (If you're lucky, a typewriter may be furnished for you to use.) *Never* complete an application in cursive; if you do, you probably won't make the paper cut. Always carry an erasable pen and your sample application in your briefcase, so you'll be prepared with the information and tools you need in case you can't bring the application home with you.

> *"Pay attention to details. Never send in an application with even one single typo!"*
> —Instructional coordinator and member of interview committee for a suburban district in Virginia

Whether you type or print your application, be sure it is error-free and has no misspelled words.

An application that has every section completed in a clear, easy-to-read way, with no typos or misspelled words, has an excellent chance of making the paper cut.

We have included two applications that were filled out by Karen McCrae (whose sample resume was included earlier in this chapter). Her first application was very poorly prepared. Not only was it handwritten, it was messy and incomplete. There were several errors, including her home address and the information about her teaching credential. Her second try was much better: neatly typed, complete, and error-free.

If you were the personnel director of a large school district, which one would you put at the top of the pile?

LAKETOWN HIGH SCHOOL
Laketown, Illinois
CERTIFICATED APPLICATION
Personnel Services: (501) 555-8000
FAX: (501) 555-8004
AN EQUAL OPPORTUNITY EMPLOYER

Regular _____
Substitute _____
Home Teaching _____

PERSONAL:

McCrae, Karen A.
Last Name   First Name   M.I.   Social Security No. *556-07-1131*

Present Address *2117 Bennington Way*   Phone *708 555-1908*
(Street)
Taylorville, ILL 60005
(City and State)   (Zip)

Permanent Address *206 Laverne Way*   Phone (*708*) *276-4415*
(Street)
Taylorville, IL 60215
(City and State)   (Zip)

POSITION DESIRED:

Level Preference: List subject and/or grade level of preference:

_____ ELEMENTARY (K-5)

☒ MIDDLE (6-8)

☒ HIGH SCHOOL (9-12)   *History, French*

_____ OTHER   *Girls' basketball/volleyball coach*

Please list other languages you speak: *Spanish/french*

ILLINOIS CREDENTIAL INFORMATION:

Expiration Date

Illinois Credentials now held *Secondary Teaching* *6/2003*

If no Illinois credential now, have you applied for one? YES _____ NO ✓

What type? _____ When? _____

Do you hold an out-of-state credential?

YES ___ NO ___ What type? _____ State _____

EDUCATION AND PROFESSIONAL TRAINING: (College or University only)

Name and Location of Institution Attended	Dates Attended From	To	Major(s)	Minor	Graduation Date – Degrees
Lincoln University Arlington Heights, IL	*9/95*	*9/98*	*History*	*French*	*1998 BA History*

TEACHING AND/OR ADMINISTRATIVE EXPERIENCE:

Total years of full-time, paid teaching experience: _____ Total years of administrative and/or supervisory experience: _____ LIST ALL EXPERIENCE BY POSITIONS IN CHRONOLOGICAL ORDER. ADMINISTRATORS NEED NOT LIST STUDENT TEACHING. FOR TEACHER APPLICANTS, LIST STUDENT TEACHING FIRST. DO NOT COUNT STUDENT TEACHING IN TOTAL YEARS TAUGHT.

Dates	Location (City/State)	Name/Level of School	Grade or Subjects Taught	Salary
1/98-5/98	*Cragmont, IL*	*Cragmont High 9-12*	*10 U.S. History 11 World History*	Student Teaching

LAKETOWN HIGH SCHOOL
Laketown, Illinois
CERTIFICATED APPLICATION
Personnel Services: (501) 555-8000
FAX: (501) 555-8004
AN EQUAL OPPORTUNITY EMPLOYER

Regular ___X___
Substitute _____
Home Teaching _____

PERSONAL:

| McCrae | Karen | A. | Social Security No. 556-07-1131 |
| Last Name | First Name | M.I. | |

Present Address __2117 Bennington Way__
(Street)

Phone (708) 555-1908

__Taylorville, Ill.__   __60005__
(City and State)   (Zip)

Permanent Address __206 Lavern Way__
(Street)

Phone (708) 276-4415

__Taylorville, Ill.__   __60215__
(City and State)   (Zip)

POSITION DESIRED:

Level Preference: List subject and/or grade level of preference:

____ ELEMENTARY (K-5) _____

____ MIDDLE (6-8) _____

_X_ HIGH SCHOOL (9-12)   __History, French__

_X_ OTHER   __Girl's basketball/Volleyball coach__

Please list other languages you speak: __Spanish / French__

ILLINOIS CREDENTIAL INFORMATION:

Expiration Date

Illinois Credentials now held _____   _____

_____   _____

If no Illinois credential now, have you applied for one? **YES** ____ **NO** ____

What type? __General Secondary__ When? __June 1998__

Do you hold an out-of-state credential?

YES ___ **NO** _X_ What type? _____ State _____

EDUCATION AND PROFESSIONAL TRAINING: (College or University only)

Name and Location of Institution Attended	Dates Attended From	To	Major(s)	Minor	Graduation Date – Degrees
Lincoln University Arlington Heights, IL	9/95	9/98	History	French	June, 1998 B.A.
Taylorville Community College Taylorville, Illinois	9/93	6/95	History	None	June, 1995 A.A.

TEACHING AND/OR ADMINISTRATIVE EXPERIENCE:

Total years of full-time, paid teaching experience: _____ Total years of administrative and/or supervisory experience: _____ LIST ALL EXPERIENCE BY POSITIONS IN CHRONOLOGICAL ORDER. ADMINISTRATORS NEED NOT LIST STUDENT TEACHING. FOR TEACHER APPLICANTS, LIST STUDENT TEACHING FIRST. DO NOT COUNT STUDENT TEACHING IN TOTAL YEARS TAUGHT.

Dates	Location (City/State)	Name/Level of School	Grade or Subjects Taught	Salary
1/98-6/98	Craymont, IL	Craymont High School 9-12	10-U.S. History 11-World History	Student Teaching
(Also coached girls' basketball; computer research)				Stud.Teach.
9/97-12/97	Newport, IL	Treyton High School	History; French; girls' volleyball	Stud. Teach.

Impressive Cover Letters

You should never send an application or a resume without a cover letter. Not all applicants know the importance of cover letters (also known as "letters of intent"), but if you take the time to include one with your application, the extra touch of professionalism will increase your chances of making the paper cut.

Here's how it works: If there are 100 applicants for one position, the first cut usually is made by the personnel director and his or her staff, especially in large school districts. This screening results in perhaps 20 files that make the first cut and are sent on to the site administrator for review. This administrator, usually the school principal, must narrow the applicants down to the top 10 or so, who will be scheduled for interviews. All else being equal, the principal will select those applicants who make the most professional presentations. An impressive cover letter will help you be one of those applicants.

Here are some general guidelines to use when composing a cover letter:

✓ The letter should be typed in original (no copies) or computer-generated and printed on a quality printer. *Never send a handwritten letter.*

✓ Use high-quality white or off-white 8 1/2" by 11" paper.

✓ Use perfect grammar.

✓ No typos or misspelled words are allowed.

✓ Never address the letter "Dear Sir," "Dear Madam," or "To Whom It May Concern." Make a telephone call to find out exactly who should receive your letter, along with the person's title and the correct spelling of the person's name.

The suggested content of the letter is shown below:

COVER LETTER/LETTER OF INTENT
CONTENT FORMAT

Your Name
Your Address

Today's Date

Name of the Administrator or Personnel Director
Name of School District
Street Address or P. O. Box
City, State, Zip Code

Dear _____ :

State the purpose of the letter (to be considered for any positions that may become available, or for a specific position that has been advertised).

Tell them what your status is now, and why you feel you would be especially well qualified for this position. (A chance to tell them about one of your strengths.)

This paragraph should include one or two brief sentences that emphasize your passion for teaching and your love for kids.

If possible, it is always nice to personalize your letter by saying something positive about the community or school district and why you would like to work there. (When you call to ask for the name of the person to whom the letter should be sent, ask if the district or city has a web address. If so, this will tell you what the city and district have to offer.)

Let them know that you have arranged to have a copy of your transcript and letters of reference forwarded to them. Thank them for their time and consideration.

Sincerely,

Your Name

Your cover letter, like any business letter, should be tailored to each specific job vacancy. The sample cover letter that follows was written by Karen McCrae, whose resume and application were included earlier. She has tailored her letter to a specific job vacancy: "High school history and social studies teacher; assistant coach—girls' varsity basketball."

Karen McCrae
2117 Bennington Way
Taylorville, IL 60005

May 3, 1998

Dr. Richard Fagan, Principal
Laketown High School
Laketown, IL 60048

Dear Dr. Fagan:

Please consider me as an applicant for the eleventh grade history/social studies position that will be available this coming fall. I learned of this vacancy from my college placement office at Lincoln University where I will earn my bachelor's degree on June 5 with a major in History and a minor in French.

I notice that your job announcement includes adjunct duties as girls' assistant basketball coach. This is of great interest to me, not only because of my past experience playing and coaching women's basketball, but because it would give me one more opportunity to fulfill my passion to make a difference in students' lives by showing them respect and building their self-esteem. When my students are my age, I want to be the one who stands out in their memories because I really cared.

Although I have visited Laketown several times, I never knew until recently of your high school's fine academic reputation. I notice that 89 percent of your graduates go on to college. The community must be very proud of its high school, and rightfully so.

I look forward to hearing from you soon and meeting with you personally at your convenience. I can be reached at (708) 555-1908.

Sincerely,

Karen McCrae

If you were Dr. Fagan and had a tall stack of applications sitting on your desk, wouldn't this well-written cover letter catch your attention? Especially if none of the other applicants had bothered to include one.

So include a cover letter whenever you are sending an application or a resume. It will help you make the paper cut.

Sterling References

You will need four to six letters of reference for your job search. Typically, these are written by people who can attest to your character and teaching ability. They are usually sent to your college or university career placement office to be included in your professional file. That way they are all together in one place, ready to be sent out on request.

You have a right to see any and all references placed in your professional file, and if there are any of questionable value, you may have them removed. Your placement office staff will help you evaluate all the letters that come in, and if it is determined that a letter is to be removed, you must follow the procedures of your placement center. An undesirable letter may be removed from your file and destroyed or it may be placed in an inactive file, where it will not be sent with your other letters of recommendation.

There are two kinds of reference letters: professional and personal.

Professional Reference Letters

Early in your career, professional letters of recommendation usually are written by people who have direct knowledge of your student teaching ability. These include college professors, college supervisors, and master teachers. As you gain experience, these letters will be replaced with new letters written by department heads, principals, superintendents, and fellow teachers.

Personal Reference Letters

Personal letters of recommendation are an important part of your file, especially when you're just getting started in your career. They generally are written by people who know you well and can share insights into your character and values. These could include former teachers, counselors, coaches, administrators, members of the clergy, neighbors, and leaders of youth organizations.

Professional letters of recommendation are written by people who are familiar with the process; they have typically written many of these letters and they know exactly what is expected in the way of content and format. This may not be the case with personal letters. When you ask someone for a personal letter of recommendation, pay careful attention to the person's response. If the person seems hesitant or isn't quite sure how to go about it, offer to furnish copies of the letters you've already received. These will be a big help in terms of wording and format.

Once your professional file is full of reference letters, it is up to you to maintain the file by periodically requesting new or updated letters of recommendation. This way your file is always fresh and up to date.

By the way, one of the biggest mistakes new teacher-candidates make is to wait until the last minute to request these reference letters. Be aware that people don't always write them on a moment's notice, even if they have the best intentions of doing so. Some procrastinate because they're on overload at the moment and don't have time to write a letter; others are forgetful or may lose your original request.

Also, it is important to remember that a professor or supervisor may have 20 other letters to write, so be considerate. And then there's always Murphy's Law, which says that when you need to reach someone the most, that person is on hiatus, traveling down the Amazon, or recovering from surgery and not due back in the office for six weeks. So make your requests as early as possible; you'll be glad you did.

Once your references are in, make a few extra copies to slip into your portfolio so you'll have them with you during your interviews. You typically won't be handing these out at interviews, or even be asked for them, but who knows? It can't hurt to have them handy.

If you pass the paper cut with your application and resume, *these letters will be requested*. Their content may determine whether you make it to the interview table or not—just one more step in the paper cut.

3

Discovering Job Vacancies

There are several ways to find out about job vacancies: Some take a bit of work; others are a matter of *"luck."* In this chapter, we'll cover some of the ways you can improve on your *"luck"* in hearing about job openings.

University Career Placement Centers

If your college or university has a placement center, you should contact the staff as soon as possible. Placement services vary greatly from one school to another. Some colleges offer no placement services at all, others provide limited services, and some have well-staffed offices with surprisingly complete services. So consider yourself lucky if yours is the full-service type.

Historically, college placement offices have given special consideration to those in the teaching profession. While first-year placement

> *Of the teacher candidates in our survey, 50 percent said they used the services of their university career placement centers.*

files may be maintained for graduates in most disciplines, many placement offices will maintain placement files for teachers during their entire careers.

If your college does not offer the services you need, check with other colleges. Some offer free services to part-time students, while others charge a reasonable fee. This latter option becomes a consideration once you've decided where you want to teach. If you're looking for a position outside your immediate area, a college in that location may have job listings not available through your own university.

A comprehensive placement program will offer several services.

✓ Schedule workshops and offer counseling on various subjects, such as these:

- How to initiate your professional file
- Job application procedures
- Ethics of the job search
- Interview techniques

The workshops usually are held in conjunction with your student teaching program, and representatives from the placement office will coordinate these activities with classroom professors during your final year at the college.

✓ Provide forms and procedures for establishing your placement file

As you establish your file as a first-year teacher, you will need to complete all the forms and follow their procedures. You also will need to provide letters of reference from professionals who observed you during your student teaching phase, including your master teacher, college supervisor, school principal, and peers at the school where you taught. It's a good idea to ask for recommendations from people outside education as well, including former employers who can attest to your work ethic, dedication, and character. You also should ask for letters from those familiar with any youth-oriented volunteer service you have performed.

Once you've landed a teaching position and have been teaching for a while, it's up to you to maintain your placement file. Keep the information current, including letters of reference from administrators and others at your school or district. In fact, ask for letters of reference every time you change positions, particularly from one school to another, or when your immediate supervisor is leaving his or her position for some reason. If you don't ask for these letters at the time, it may be difficult to get them later.

The important thing to remember is that future employers will want to know who you are and what you've done *lately,* not what you did 10 years ago. A good rule of thumb is this: Unless a letter of reference can tell about something you've done that has "significantly altered the course of humankind," let it pass into your inactive file after several years and replace it with a current letter.

✓ Maintain a job-related reference library

These libraries may contain information on schools throughout the world, including addresses, officials to contact, hiring procedures, and salary information. Particularly helpful are state school directories for the entire United States and some of the larger individual school districts. All of these directories contain valuable information for job seekers.

✓ Maintain lists of current educational job vacancies

New job openings usually are posted on the placement office's bulletin board or added to a large three-ring binder. Some placement centers also send a weekly or monthly job listing to your home, if you are willing to pay a subscription fee. Listings are generally for the immediate area around the college or university, but often you will see expanded lists of openings throughout the state, the country, and the world.

✓ Notify candidates of interview schedules for recruitment teams from visiting school districts

School district personnel may visit college campuses to recruit teachers. The frequency of these visits is determined by the job market and funding. If jobs are plentiful and teachers scarce, expect to see more on-campus recruiting. If school districts have adequate funding, they expand their labor pool by searching college campuses for the best possible talent. Conversely, if teachers are in great supply or the districts are short on funds, don't expect to see many recruiters on campus. The number of on-campus interviews varies from year to year.

✓ Send your professional file to appropriate school districts

Most college placement offices will send your professional file to school districts, but you need to familiarize yourself with your college's procedures. Some want the teacher-candidate to initiate the request, while others want the request to come from school district personnel. Some colleges offer this service for free, while others charge a fee.

If your college offers placement services, be sure to contact them early, fill out their forms as neatly and accurately as possible, and follow all their rules. And always be on the lookout for anyone who may write a sterling reference to include in your professional file.

Job Fairs

> *In our survey, 37 percent of the teacher-candidates said they attended job fairs in their pursuit of teaching positions.*

When it comes to job fairs, it appears that the exception *is* the rule. While formats and sponsors vary greatly, however, there is a single purpose for these fairs: to get job seekers together with prospective employers.

Here are the most frequent sponsors of educational job fairs:

✓ Large school districts

Far and away the biggest sponsors of job fairs are the larger school districts. For a variety of reasons, larger districts are constantly in search of new teachers, and educational job fairs are one of the many ways they recruit these teachers.

✓ County offices of education

Another frequent sponsor of educational job fairs are county offices of education. One of the primary functions of these offices is to provide services and expertise to smaller schools within their counties, and job fairs provide a simple way to introduce teachers to these schools.

✓ College placement centers

Many college placement offices organize their own job fairs, at which several schools, districts, and county offices of education are represented.

✓ Individual schools

You will occasionally find individual schools that set up booths at general job fairs. A general job fair includes a variety of corporate and governmental employers who are searching for employees with many different majors and degrees.

The format for educational job fairs varies. A teaching candidate may find school representatives actively screening files and conducting interviews for actual vacancies—and even hiring on the spot. More commonly, however, the representatives collect files and conduct informal interviews with the goal of placing candidates in a hiring pool for consideration at a later date. Each school's or district's representative conducts a "show and tell" promotion, encouraging candidates to consider employment with that school or district.

> *"We hire about 50 percent of our teachers from job fairs and through university placement offices. The rest are hired through referrals from other teachers and administrators, unsolicited resumes, and from our substitute teacher pool."*
>
> —Bilingual resource specialist and member of interview committee for a large, urban school district in California

While educational job fairs can occur any time during the year, the vast majority happen between January and July. Watch for announcements of these fairs in your local newspaper and on the bulletin board of your college placement office. You can also call various county offices of education or specific school districts and ask if they have fairs scheduled.

We encourage you to participate in at least one large educational job fair in your area. This is a valuable way to sell yourself to prospective employers.

Whenever you attend a job fair, be sure to bring along extra copies of your resume, college placement file, evidence of teaching certificates, demonstration video, your portfolio, and a list of questions to ask each representative. Your personal appearance is important, so dress the same way you would for a formal, scheduled interview.

After each job fair, send thank-you notes to the representatives of any schools or districts where you plan to formally pursue employment.

School Surveys

School surveys are a smart way to discover job vacancies before they're advertised and to shop yourself around. They also provide a way for discovering which schools are a "fit" for you—which dovetail with your mission statement. These surveys are conducted in person, as cold calls. You simply drop by the offices of any schools or districts that interest you, whether they have any current vacancies or not.

> *"A wise man will make more opportunities than he finds."*
> —*Francis Bacon*

*Note: These calls should be made **in person**, not over the telephone.*

Although only 13 percent of the teacher-candidates we talked with conducted school surveys, we think they are *a must*. Here's why.

While almost all teaching vacancies must, by law, be advertised, you're at a great advantage if you know about them ahead of time. There are other ways to find them, of course—through networking (which we'll talk about later in this chapter) or by being in the right place at the right time. But one excellent way to hear of vacancies before they're advertised is to conduct your own school surveys.

Here is how to go about it:

1. **Make a list of the school districts and specific schools that interest you.**

By this time you probably have some idea of the schools at which you might like to teach. Maybe you heard about them from your professors, friends, or relatives; or maybe you really liked the school where you did your student teaching. One consideration is driving distance from your home. Only you know how far you are willing to drive to work each day, or if you're willing to make a move to another city.

Be sure to consider *all* the schools in your area. There may be schools you are not familiar with, or private or religious schools you might consider, as well. Or you may hear of a school through your network. The important thing is that you don't limit yourself only to those schools with the "friendly faces," people you already know or have met. Most of your contacts will be cold calls, and *that's okay!* By leaving your comfort zone and reaching beyond the friendly faces, you'll uncover openings your competitors haven't heard about.

2. **Once you've made your list, organize it by placing your first choices at the top.**

You will need to keep a record of your contacts. Use the form on the next page as a guide; you will need one sheet per school or district.

Later in the chapter you will notice we include "school report cards." These are also known as a school's "Annual Report to the Community." This sheet of information tells about the school's mission statement, philosophy, ethnic profile, test scores, attendance records, expenditures per student, class sizes, facilities, services offered, teacher evaluation policies, discipline policies, textbooks and instructional materials used, and salaries.

Not all schools offer this kind of information to the public, but many states require that schools make these reports available. If you can get your hands on one of these report cards for each school you visit, you'll have a world of information at your fingertips. We have included two school report cards, one from a high school and one from an elementary school.

School Survey

Name of school or district: _____

Address: _____

Telephone number: _____

Date of first contact: _____

Name and title of the person you contacted: _____

Upcoming vacancies (if any): _____

_____

What did you receive from the school or district? _____

_____

School report card? _____

District brochure? _____

Notices of current vacancies? _____

An application? _____

Other? _____

What did you give them? _____

Resume? _____

Letters of reference? _____

Demo video? _____

Other? _____

Follow up:

Second visit? _____

_____

_____

Date: _____

Name and title of person you contacted: _____

Returned application? _____ Date: _____

Had college placement file sent: _____ Date: _____

Other follow-up contacts: _____

Your comments and impressions of the school/district: _____

_____

_____

District brochures can be very revealing, as well. Later in this chapter we have included a sample brochure from Mt. Diablo Unified School District in California.

Sample High School Report Card

Tempe Unified School District

Tempe High School Report Card
An Annual Report to the Community
1996-1997 School Year

John Rogers, Principal   Fall 1995

MISSION STATEMENT/GOALS

"We will enable each student to realize his/her potential, achieve self-sufficiency, and be a responsible citizen."

Our school-wide instructional goals include the development of the intellectual disciplines, mental and physical health, economic and vocational competence, citizenship and civic responsibility.

SCHOOL PHILOSOPHY

Tempe High believes in the worth and the dignity of the individual student.

We believe in the importance of pursuing the truth and knowledge, a commitment to excellence, and the nurturing of responsible citizenship.

We believe that growth and change should be responsible to the needs of the students, staff, community and the nation.

We believe in the democratic process in the sense that we involve students, staff, parents, and members of the community in the decision-making process, constantly striving to achieve the mission statement and goals established for our students, school, and district.

BUSINESS/SCHOOL PARTNERSHIPS

THS has business/school partnerships with PG&E, TriCounties Bank, Express Personnel, and Primerica Financial Services. THS is also a participant in an academic incentive program with the Tempe Rotary Club called "Achievement Builds Choice."

Parents actively participate in the decision-making process through the following school committees: School Site Council, PTSA, VEA Advisory Councils, Administrative Council, Ag Advisory Council, Business Advisory Council, and Bilingual Advisory Council. Joining our school this year are Tempe High West and ACT Advisory Boards. Parents also support the school by participating in athletic and music booster groups.

SCHOOL PROFILE

Tempe High School, established in 1902 and adjacent to the Tempe State University, is a four year comprehensive high school and is one of five secondary schools in the Tempe Unified School District.

THS is accredited by the Western Association of Schools and Colleges for a term of six years, the highest term of accreditation given. Our current enrollment is approximately 1,910 students. We are a School Improvement Program (SIP) school, the first high school in Northern Wyoming awarded a state grant to improve the curriculum reflecting the needs and desires of the students, parents, teachers and administration.

THS was designated in 1989 as a National Exemplary High School by the U.S. Department of Education. We were one of only 107 public high schools across our nation designated for this prestigious award. THS continues to strive for excellence in all phases of our operations.

THS has created two "schools within a school" Tempe High West and The Academy of Communications Technology (ACT) to offer students, parents, and staff an educational option to a traditional high school .

ETHNIC PROFILE

Our school population is comprised of students from many different countries and various ethnic backgrounds. The ethnic profile of the school follows:

Caucasian	70.5%
Hispanic	14.2%
Asian	9.2%
African American	2.9%
American Indian	2.0%
Others	1.2%

STUDENT ACHIEVEMENT

Last fall, Tempe High School's eleventh grade students took the Stanford Achievement Test in reading, language, and mathematics. , The results follow:

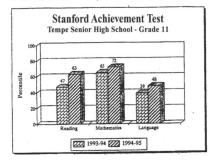

TEACHER ASSIGNMENT

All members of the Tempe High School certificated staff have fulfilled the requirements for a teaching credential as regulated by the Wyoming Teaching Credential Department. There are full-time equivalent teachers at Tempe High School. All are teaching within their area of authorization. Thirty percent (30%) of the certificated teaching staff have masters degrees or higher.

STUDENT ATTENDANCE AND COMPLETION RATES

District produced data indicates that the average daily attendance for the past three years at our school site has been:

1992-1993	97.24%
1993-1994	96.78%
1994-1995	97.27%

A intervention tool designed to help students stay in school implemented for this school is a tutor/detention program. Students who demonstrate behaviors which directly effect school performance i.e. truancy, tardies etc. are assigned to an academic tutor after school in place of traditional detention. Other intervention programs include, but are not limited to, Student Study Team intervention, Ninth Grade Summer Counseling, At-risk counseling, a Title I Instructional program, special alcohol and drug counseling, a Saturday Alternative Program, partnership programs with local businesses, student recognition programs, and individual and group counseling.

New to Tempe High this year is a School Truancy Officer who will work with students and parents with severe attendance concerns.

EXPENDITURES PER STUDENT

For the 1996-1997 school year our district will spend an average of $3,506 per student excluding categorical programs and lottery expenditures.

In addition to these general funds, we receive supplemental funding for purposes as specified:

Source	$Funding
Athletics	16,115
Agriculture (State)	14,533
Bilingual Instruction (State)	64,311
Gifted & Talented Instruction (State)	968
Music	6,221
Special Education (State)	7,108
School Improvement (State)	94,414
Textbook Funds (State)	*28,200
10th Grade Counseling (State)	8,205
Title I (Federal)	92,000
Title VI - Library (Federal)	8,372

CLASS SIZE

The District staffs each secondary school at a 33:1 student/teacher ratio. Additionally, Tempe High School receives supplemental staffing for special education instruction, agriculture, and work experience. As of September 1995, the average class size for English, mathematics, science, and social science was as follows:

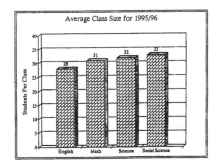

To offset the student/teacher ratio and to provide additional support for teachers and students, the School Site Council has employed parent aides in English, science, and the computer labs. The state has provided additional monies to our district to lower academic class sizes. We have chosen to reduce sophomore English class size to a 1:20 teacher/student ratio.

SCHOOL FACILITIES AND SAFETY

Four additional portable classrooms were added for 1996-1997 school year in addition to the 7 existing portables. In addition to the four existing computer labs, an additional computer lab to support

ACT and History/ Social Science, as well as four new computers which will be going into the Science Wing All computers are connected by a fiber optic local area network with access to a wide area network and the World Wide Web.

As a reward for excellent academic performance, we are continuing to offer a reserved parking area for students with a 4.0 GPA within our faculty parking lot. Excellent custodial, grounds, and maintenance staff do an effective job of keeping the facilities clean and maintained. Maintaining this standard is an area of concern as continued budget cuts are having an adverse impact on our facilities.

Our school has an emergency plan, and evacuation procedures are practiced as per state law. THS has had an asbestos survey and an abatement plan developed.

Tempe High School was commended in the recent WASC accreditation study for providing a "friendly, positive, safe, and secure environment that fosters a high degree of trust, respect, and cooperation among an increasingly ethnically diverse student population." *(WASC School Report,* p. 58)

COUNSELING AND STUDENT SUPPORT SERVICES

Student support services at THS include 4.2 counselors, a.6 bilingual/Title I counselor, a psychologist (three days per week), a school nurse (two days per week), a full-time health aide, and a full-time librarian.

The case load for school counselors is 400:1. Outside agencies provide services to students through Child Protective Services Homeless Emergency Runaway Effort, Migrant Education, Mini Corps, Pomac County Mental Health Youth Treatment Services, TSU/C tutors, Teen Parent Services, private practice psychologists, Tempe Community Hospital Crossroads, Pomac Memorial Hospital Stress and Health Center, Parent Education Network, Children's Home Society, Tempe State University, Tempe, Upward Bound, American Indian Education Program, and the Pomac Communicatively Handicapped programs.

Tempe School has a Career Center available to students throughout the school day. Students may take career awareness and vocational aptitude assessments on a scheduled basis.

TEACHER EVALUATION

To assist in maintaining quality instructional practices, tenured teachers are evaluated on their teaching performance a minimum of every other year. Beginning teachers are evaluated annually. Site administrators within the Tempe Unified School District have been trained and certified as competent evaluators. Major areas evaluated are Pupil Progress, Learning Environment, Student Control, Other Duties, and Support Services.

Teachers are provided opportunities to participate in staff development activities to maintain and improve their professional skills through site and district staff development plans, as well as through independent staff efforts. Tempe High School is fortunate to have so many fine and dedicated teachers.

CLASSROOM DISCIPLINE AND CLIMATE FOR LEARNING

We believe our school climate is a strength, and we are proud of how well our students interrelate with one another and with our staff. Tempe High School has developed and practices a clear and consistent discipline plan. A booklet titled, "A Guide to School Discipline" is provided for each student at the beginning of the school year. It outlines the consequences for student misbehavior. Students are encouraged to mediate disputes and are taught appropriate conflict resolution techniques. Student suspensions are used as a last resort in the discipline process.

If students feel safe and good about themselves, they tend to perform better academically and socially. Our school has a wide variety of academic and extra-curricular activities available to challenge and encourage students. Students can participate in over thirty-eight-curricular clubs and thirty-two different athletic teams. In the recent WASC accreditation study, students were commended for "their school pride, spirit, behavior, and appreciation for the differences among them" (WASC *School Report,* p. 58)

Routinely students receive awards such as Academic Student of the Quarter, academic block letters, and athletic block letters. Last year THS students were awarded approximately $350,000 in scholarships to further their education beyond high school.

STAFF TRAINING AND CURRICULUM IMPROVEMENT

Our school is committed to staff training and curriculum improvement. This school year all staff will participate in six in-service sessions on August 25, October 2, October 27, January 26, April 8, and May 28. Staff members also have the opportunity to participate in workshops and in-service programs specific to their subject matter.

This year's focus for staff development is on instructional technology, campus safety, school-wide learning environment, and multi-cultural understanding. Curriculum improvement also is a high priority with the school staff. We also devote a great deal of time and energy to see that our curriculum is appropriately aligned with the standards of the state frameworks.

SUBSTITUTE TEACHERS

The Tempe Unified School District maintains an abundant pool of highly qualified and talented substitute teachers available to insure the continuance of a quality instructional program at both the elementary and secondary levels.

TEXTBOOKS AND INSTRUCTIONAL MATERIALS

Tempe High School follows TUSD procedures for adopting textbooks, a process which includes teacher, student and administrative recommendations. The Board of Education has the final responsibility for adopting all textbooks in our district.

Our Library Media Center is a comprehensive information technology center with an automated library, computer and career centers, and a video production area. The collection includes approximately 17,000 books, over 100 periodical titles, and a variety of computer and audiovisual programs. The School Based Coordinated Program (SBCP) has supported the Library Media Center by funding parent aides for the Career/ Computer Center and Instructional Media programs. In addition, SBCP has expanded LMC Computer Center for individual, class, and staff use.

QUALITY OF INSTRUCTION AND LEADERSHIP

Tempe High School's teaching and support staff is competent, dedicated, and sensitive to student needs.

Our school has been nationally recognized primarily because of the outstanding people who work here.

The WASC accreditation team commended "The staff for their caring attitudes, accessibility, and flexibility addressing the academic, social and emotional needs of students." (WASC School Report, pp.46, 52-58)

The school has been reorganized into two school teams to provide more personal service to students. An assistant principal, two counselors, and an attendance clerk provide support services and are responsible for the academic growth, attendance, and other needs of the students on their team. A School Site Council has the' responsibility of allocating SBCP monies on an annual basis. Student Government, PTSA, and Instructional and Administrative Council are additional examples of shared decision making groups.

THS is proud of the many staff members who are leaders of organizations, mentor teachers, and representatives to various boards and charitable organizations. The high standard of student achievement at THS is directly related to the high quality of instruction and leadership at our school.

Our instructional program is consistent with state and local board directives. Our programs are externally and internally reviewed on a regular basis. The staff has the desire to update and improve the offerings as the priorities of our nation, state, and district change as evidenced by the addition of Tempe High West and ACT, as well as Humanities: Arts and Ideas, a new instructional model for integrating art history and activities with English. In the last state program quality review the following departments were commended as model programs: English/Language Arts, Foreign Language, Science, and Visual and Performing Arts.

SALARY INFORMATION

Salary Category (1993/94)	TUSD Annual Salary Schedule	TUSD Daily Pay	Comparison State Annual Salary Schedule	Comparison State Range Pay	Comparison State Range Annual Salary
Teachers					
Beginning	$27,281	$148	$26,221	$143	$20,285–$29,500
Mid-Range	36,591	199	40,480	221	34,654–44,876
Highest	49,807	271	49,398	270	44,948–57,250
Principals (Average)*	62,297	298	65,403	309	54,416–71,324
Superintendent	88,000	400	96,815	432	79,462–120,000
Budget Percentage (1993/94)					
Teachers' Salaries	43.98%		43.51%		38.17%–47.19%
Administrative	6.03%		5.42%		4.02–7.90%

*TUSD data includes 21 Principals

**TUSD data includes Superintendent and two Assistant Superintendents

Sample Elementary School Report Card

Tempe Unified School District

Clayborne Elementary School Report Card
An Annual Report to the Community
1996-1997 School Year

Benjamin Nelson, Principal   Fall 1996

SCHOOL PROFILE

Clayborne School is located on the northeast side of Tempe in an older section of town. The school itself is in the city limits, but all homes surrounding it are located outside of the city limits. The attendance area includes families from as far west as 17th Avenue, and to the east it extends to Highway 70.

The enrollment for kindergarten through sixth grade is 820 students. Our students come from a wide variety of ethnic backgrounds (i.e. , American Indian, Asian, Hispanic, and Black). This represents approximately 66% of our enrollment.

The Clayborne School ethnicity profile is:

Hispanic	36.6%
Caucasian	33.7%
Asian	24.4%
Black	4.7%
American Indian	0.3%
Other	0.3%

We have 426 students that have a dominant language other than English (i.e., Spanish, Hmong, Laotian, Cambodian, Vietnamese, German, and Tigrna).

The enrollment of the school has grown from 580 in the 1985-86 school year to the present 721. This is a large increase in nine years. Clayborne school is on a four track year-round schedule. Two of the four tracks are Spanish Bilingual.

TEACHER ASSIGNMENT

There are 41 teachers at Clayborne School. All teach within their areas of authorization. In addition to the 33 classroom teachers we have one Fine Arts/Music Teacher, two Special Day Class Teachers, one Resource Specialist teacher, one E.S.L. teacher, one Title I Resource teacher and a Reading Recovery Teacher.

STUDENT ATTENDANCE INFORMATION

Research indicates that school attendance is a major indicator of student achievement. Clayborne School's attendance rate for the past three years has been:

1992-93	98.19%
1993-94	97.98%
1994-95	98.08%

The school has implemented several intervention programs that are designed to keep our absence rate low. The following programs were designed to alert the school of problems and to help remedy them: Student Study Team, P.E.N. Counseling, Primary Intervention Program, School Attendance and Review Board, school attendance awards, Project C.L.A.S.S. and Project S.E.L.F. (self esteem programs), "Here's Looking at You 2000," School Watch (Tempe PD), D.A.R.E.

EXPENDITURES PER STUDENT

Tempe Unified School District spends an average of $3,506 per student from the general fund. In addition to these general fund monies, Clayborne School receives supplemental funding for specific purposes. A school Based Coordinated Program budget of $180,200 supports our school improvement effort, and the Title I budget of $262,327 provides extra services and materials for students needing extra help (based upon student test scores). The Title I and School Based Coordinated Program funds are budgeted by our School Site Council, with approximately 2/3 of the money being used to fund classroom aides who provide extra help for students.

The federally funded Title VI budget is used to purchase library books totaling $3,563.

TEXTBOOKS & INSTRUCTIONAL MATERIALS

Updated and readily available resources are important if students are to perform at their best in **class.** The State of Wyoming adopts textbooks that meet quality standards established by the State Board of Education. The Tempe Unified School District selects textbooks and other instructional materials from these state adoptions in a seven year cycle; moving from math to reading, to science, etc... All of the textbooks currently in use meet these standards and were selected to match the needs of Clayborne students by committees of teachers' and administrators. Clayborne School maintains a Resource Center where many language arts and math materials are catalogued and stored for teacher use.

This year our school budgeted $5,474 for new library books. Our library maintains approximately 14 books for every student. In addition, a librarian aide was employed to organize and run the school library along with many parent volunteer hours.

SUBSTITUTE TEACHERS

Tempe Unified School District is extremely fortunate to have an abundant pool of highly qualified and talented substitute teachers available to insure the continuance of a quality instructional program at both the elementary and secondary levels.

SALARY AND BUDGET INFORMATION

School districts must provide salary comparison information in their School Report Cards. Below is a chart comparing T.U.S.D. with the rest of the state.

Salary Category (1993/94)	TUSD Annual Salary Schedule	TUSD Daily Pay	Comparison State Annual Salary Schedule	Comparison State Range Pay	Comparison State Range Annual Salary
Teachers					
Beginning	$27,281	$148	$26,221	$143	$20,285–$29,500
Mid-Range	36,591	199	40,480	221	34,654–44,876
Highest	49,807	271	49,398	270	44,948–57,250
Principals (Average)*	62,297	298	65,403	309	54,416–71,324
Superintendent	88,000	400	96,815	432	79,462–120,000
Budget Percentage (1993/94)					
Teachers' Salaries	43.98%		43.51%		38.17%–47.19%
Administrative	6.03%		5.42%		4.02–7.90%

*TUSD data includes 21 Principals

TRAINING AND CURRICULUM IMPROVEMENT

The teaching staff participates in six inservice days yearly designed to improve teaching skills. Specific areas include: Language Arts, Science, Math, multicultural Education and Technology. Classified Staff receive inservice on topics related to their varied roles. Additionally staff members attend workshops and conferences in selected curriculum areas throughout the school year.

Curricular improvement is an ongoing process at Clayborne which is coordinated with the entire T.U.S.D. Staff members participated in the following district-wide curricular task forces: Language Arts, Math, P.E., Science, and Health. Currently the emphasis is on implementing the new T. U. S. D. Science curriculum. A recommendation has also been made for our new math adoption.

QUALITY OF INSTRUCTION AND LEADERSHIP

Educational research clearly states the need for strong instructional leadership in an effective school. This leadership comes from the principal, assistant principal, staff, and support groups. Our School Site Council, made up of parents and staff members, provides leadership through the development of a school plan and the budgeting of funds to implement the plan. The Bilingual Advisory Committee, made up, of parents and staff, provides input and guidance to our bilingual program. in the spring of 1989, a program review was conducted by the State Department of Education. Clayborne School was commended in many areas for our effective program for students. Leadership is also provided by our high quality instructional staff. During the School Review in 1993, the staff was commended for their use of core literature in Language Arts, Clayborne's Learning Environment, the Collaboration Program, the exemplary Spanish Bilingual Program, and the Visual and Performing Arts Program.

Clayborne School was also designated a Wyoming state Compensatory Education Achieving School in the spring of 1994. Clayborne won this honor again in 1995, along with National Recognition.

CLASS SIZE

The average class size at Clayborne School is currently 25 students per class, The district's goal is to staff at a district wide average not to exceed 30. This compares favorably with other districts in Wyoming.

Tempe Unified is a growing district and space is at a premium. Progress towards reducing class size has been hindered as the state has not provided funding to do 90. Something Clayborne School has done to ease the size of classes is to employ classroom aides to lower the adult-to student ratio.

STUDENT ACHIEVEMENT

All second and fifth grade students took the Stanford Achievement Test in the fall of 1993. The results are compared to national norms across the United States. Below are graphs showing how Clayborne students scored in the areas of reading, mathematics and written language. The graphs are shown using percentile rankings.

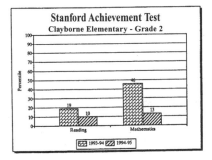

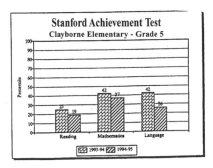

SCHOOL FACILITIES AND SAFETY

The original Clayborne School building is forty years old, having been built in 1953. In 1989 this section of the school was remodeled with state reconstruction funds. As enrollment has increased over the years, the school has expanded from the original ten classrooms to its current size of twenty-eight classrooms. Since 1986 there have been ten relocatable classrooms erected on the campus to house the growing enrollment. Clayborne School implemented a year-round education program to maximize facility utilization in July of 1990.

A school disaster plan has been developed which includes emergency procedures in case of fire, earthquake or other disaster.

CLASSROOM DISCIPLINE AND CLIMATE FOR LEARNING

Students who feel good about themselves and have opportunities to receive recognition tend to perform better academically and socially. The Student Council at Clayborne School is very active, organizing noon intramurals, student spirit activities, School Carnival, and Family Fun Night.

Students are taught the behavioral expectations in the first weeks of school with a written copy of the discipline plan sent home to parents in the Parent/Student Handbook. Appropriate playground behavior is recognized with "Clayborne Top Cat" awards. Inappropriate behavior is recognized with citations.

Students who choose to follow classroom and playground rules are recognized monthly in citizenship assemblies. The P.T.A. budgets funds to provide various incentives for good behavior.

Clayborne School has a positive learning environment and the staff has high academic expectations. In addition to recognizing good behavior, students are recognized for academic achievements through the Clayborne Honor Roll and by displaying their work.

TEACHER EVALUATION

Tenured teachers are evaluated on their teaching performance a minimum of every other year to assist them in maintaining the quality of their instructional practices. Beginning teachers are evaluated annually. Site administrators within the Tempe Unified School District have been trained and certified as competent evaluators. Major areas evaluated are Pupil Progress, Learning Environment, Student Control, Instructional Strategies and Methods, Teacher Goals and objectives, other Duties and Support Services.

Teachers are provided with numerous opportunities to participate in staff development activities to improve and maintain their professional skills. Each year the School Site Council sets aside money to provide for staff development.

COUNSELING AND STUDENT SUPPORT SERVICES

Positions providing student support services at Clayborne School include: a school psychologist, a school nurse, a health aide, a librarian aide, two Mini Corp aides, a Migrant Education aide, an American Indian Education aide, a Refugee aide and many T.S.U.C. C.A.V.E. aides and student teachers.

Clayborne school also operates a Reading and Math Learning Lab (Apple House) that serves over 280 students weekly, providing extra help through collaboration. Special Education services for students include: Speech, Resource Specialist, and two Special Day Classes.

We employ a full time counseling intern through the Parent Education Network to provide small group counseling. We have a Guidance Associate working in the Primary Intervention Program that provides guidance services for primary aged students and their parents.

Clayborne received a Healthy Start Grant from the State of Wyoming to explore ways of more 'fully providing a "healthy start" in school for our students. In addition, we received an "Even Start" grant which allows us to provide more parent education opportunities through our school.

The Clayborne Scholarship Program was implemented in the fall of 1988. Students participate in a fund-raiser that enables pupils attending Clayborne school to avail themselves of many extra curricular activities that include recreational and cultural opportunities.

Sample District Brochure

REWARDS

Mt. Diablo educators are recognized academic leaders statewide and nationally. Teachers are encouraged to expand their personal horizons and their innovative ideas are welcome.

Mt. Diablo teachers are involved in textbook selections, staff development, and program development. They are our most **valued** asset in creating program changes to meet the diverse economic, social, and academic needs of today and of the 21st century.

We invite you to share our efforts to build a batter world.

Certificated Personnel Office
Mt. Diablo Unified School District
1936 Carlotta Drive
Concord, CA 94519

Fax (510) 676-4092

COMMUNITY

• Mediterranean climate
• Suburbia benefits of rural and city living

Regional Center for Performing Arts
Concord Pavilion
San Francisco Opera and Symphony
The A's - The Giants
The 49ers - The Warriors
Windsurfing - Water skiing
Downhill and cross-country skiing
Bike and hiking trails
Deep sea and delta fishing
Golfing
Sailing - boating
Wine country
Historic Gold Country
BART - Bay Area Rapid Transit

• Opportunities for graduate study:

University of California
Stanford University
St. Mary's College
John E Kennedy University
Cal State University, Hayward
University of San Francisco
San Francisco State University
University of Pacific
Chapman College
National University

SCHOOLS

Elementary	26
Middle	9
High School, Comprehensive	6
High School, Continuation	1
Necessary Small High School	6
Special Education Centers	3

Mt. Diablo Unified School District has approximately 1600 teachers serving more than 31,000 students with a staff of 4,000 employees.

Mt. Diablo Unified School District serves students in:

Concord
Pleasant Hill
Clayton
West Pittsburg
Martinez
Pacheco
Walnut Creek

MT. DIABLO UNIFIED SCHOOL DISTRICT

We invite you to share our efforts to build a better world.

OPPORTUNITY

- A competitive salary schedule based on training and experience
- A contract including provision for personal illness, personal business, family bereavement
- Additional compensation above the salary schedule for a wide range of extracurricular, coaching, and other related assignments
- Tax sheltered annuity programs
- An orientation program for teachers new to the school district
- Comprehensive medical, dental and vision plans
- California State Teachers Retirement System
- Largest school district in Contra Costa County
- Extensive professional growth opportunities

SPECIAL ED.

- *Comprehensive programs across the full continuum of severe and nonsevere disabilities including:*
  - special day classes
  - resource specialist services
  - resource group instruction
  - small group instruction
  - speech therapy
  - adapted physical education
  - vision services
  - career/vocational services
  - counseling
  - interpretive services
  - parent education
  - community based instruction
- *Serving with emphasis on:*
  - ages 0-21
  - all disabling conditions
  - thorough collaboration/consultation
  - community/parent involvement
  - professional staff development
  - paraprofessional assistance
- *With innovations in:*
  - special education core curriculum
  - life skills curriculum
  - computer assisted IEP process
  - differential competency testing

PROGRAMS

- School business partnership
- Drug Free Education
- Site Base Staff Development
- Gifted and Talented
- Vocational Education
- ROP
- Future Business Leaders of America
- Future Homemakers of America
- Future Teachers of America
- Career Centers
- Alternative Education
- Learning Opportunities Programs
- Drop Out Prevention Programs
- Elementary Academic Advisors
- Adult Education
- School Age Mothers
- Home Study, K-8

BILINGUAL

The District's goals are to provide exemplary programs that ensure the development of English fluency and equal educational opportunities that produce empowered learners.

- Increase of bilingual classes K-12
- Transitional programs
- Primary language core programs
- English language development
- Sheltered content classes
- Curriculum development opportunities
- Diversity of 57 languages
- Staff development provided by district
- School-based coordinated programs
- New teacher support group

3. Set up a cold-calling schedule.

If you're like the rest of us, you procrastinate. Even if you agree that it's smart to conduct school surveys as part of your job search, it will take discipline to get yourself out there, pounding the pavement—especially as it means getting dressed and groomed for a possible live interview. So we suggest that you set up a calling schedule of so many cold calls per week. If you hope to start teaching in the fall, for example, you should begin your schedule in early spring, methodically calling on schools or district offices. And don't give up if your first call doesn't produce a job lead; keep going back until your face is indelibly engraved on the minds of your contacts at each school. You never know, a position may even become vacant at the very last minute, even after the school year has started, so never give up.

4. Begin making your calls.

Although cold calling may be intimidating to you, you should realize that people are *happy* to talk to you, to brag about their school or district. Every-one—including the school secretary, the custodian, teachers' aides, bus drivers, teachers, administrators, and those who

> *"Starting in March or April a candidate should make contact with every district she can conceive of working at. This process of cold calling, sending resumes, and following up continues through the end of September . . . openings pop up constantly. The individual who sends the fax first, after finding out about a position before it has been advertised, wins points for eagerness."*
>
> —*A high school music teacher in New Jersey*

work in the personnel office—will be impressed with your eagerness to become known and to find out more about them. One of the main reasons for conducting school surveys is to *become known*—you want to become a familiar face.

You will find that the more cold calls you make, the easier they become and the more encouraged you'll be. Some of your calls may result in an informal visit with the principal or personnel director. Or you may be given the name of someone else to contact, perhaps at the district office. In any case, keep in mind that your ultimate goal is to make personal contact with someone who has *hiring power.* Although your first contact will usually be with a school secretary or someone who works at the district office of personnel, ask to speak with the principal, personnel director, or anyone who sits on the hiring panel.

Make your calls with the expectation of talking to one of these key people that day. This means you should treat the process in much the same way you would a scheduled interview. That is, be prepared to make a good impression when it comes to your dress, grooming, body language, eye contact, hand shake, and attitude (we'll talk more about this in chapter 6). This isn't a formal interview, however, and you should be prepared to explain the purpose of your visit.

Here's an example of what you might say:

> *"My name is   and I'm looking for a position as a class-room teacher. I'm interested in your school district because of its excellent reputation. I plan to apply for any positions that become available, but today I was just hoping to meet you personally and learn more about your school district."*

By cold calling in advance of job announcements and meeting the principal (or anyone else who sits on the hiring panel), you are guaranteed to impress. Many of the administrators we interviewed said that when it came time to schedule interviews, they remembered which candidates had made the early calls, and they were able to put faces with the names on those applications.

By the way, it's a good idea to bring your portfolio along on these calls, just in case you're given a chance to "show and tell." Also have one of your demo videos handy, and offer to leave it with anyone who will agree to take it.

Remember, the purpose of a school survey is two-fold: Not only are you looking for a school that's a perfect fit for you but, equally as important, you're trying to become *known*. You've probably heard the expression, "It's who you know that matters." Every contact you make through cold calling enlists another important person who now *knows* you.

It keeps coming back to the Madison Avenue idea of marketing and selling your product—*you!*

> *"Pound the pavement... it gets your name out there."*
>
> —Kindergarten teacher in Washington

Network! Network! Network!

Networking has become more than a buzz word in today's corporate job market; it is now essential for job applicants to get their "net" working in every way possible. To do this, you should talk to anyone and everyone, anytime and anywhere, in the hope of discovering a job vacancy or making contact with someone who has hiring authority.

This concept has been adopted in the field of education over the past decade or so, along with other job search strategies borrowed from the corporate world (such as the use of a portfolio and a demo video). When it comes to networking, however, teachers have an advantage over those in many other professions because of the built-in network that exists in the educational community.

For example, by the time you've completed your student teaching, you will already have a net full of influential contacts: professors, school principals, mentor teachers, master teachers, and other teachers with whom you have worked.

And if you've been working on your school surveys, you have an excellent network of contacts there, as well.

> *In our survey, 51 percent of the teacher-candidates networked throughout their communities in their search of job leads and contacts.*

Many teacher-candidates have done some substitute teaching, resulting in even more contacts. If you distinguish yourself during your substitute or student teaching experiences, many of your contacts will be happy to recommend you to a "hire" authority or apprise you of upcoming openings.

If you are introduced to an administrator or personnel director, treat the meeting as you would a school survey. You may not be involved in an official interview at this meeting, but your purpose is to let this person know who you are and that you are interested in any future openings. Even if nothing is available at the moment, you never know when a position will open up in the future. At that time, you may be invited back for a formal interview. At the very least you can say that someone with the authority and power to hire you now knows who you are. The networking contacts you establish within the educational community are invaluable—treasure them!

Network outside of the educational community, as well, through face-to-face contacts and the liberal use of the telephone, voice mail, e-mail, and fax machines. Ask everyone you come into contact with if they know someone with hiring power in the local schools, or if they know of an upcoming teaching vacancy. If you make it a

> *"Talk to everyone you know or meet who is in the field of education about your job search."*
> —*A high school English teacher in Texas*

> *The more people you meet and talk to about teaching vacancies, the more chances you have of landing a job.*

point to network with people every single day, you'll be surprised at the leads you turn up. For example, you might be paired with someone at the golf course who happens to be a member of the school board, or your teller at the bank might know of an opening at her daughter's school.

Talk to everyone: members of your church, your dentist, your fellow health-nuts at the fitness club. Although we don't recommend it, we know one teacher who even customized the message on her answering machine:

"This is Cindy, the desperate, out-of-work teacher. Leave all your job-leads at the beep."

It's a statistical fact that more people find jobs through networking than they do through conventional job search methods. It's true when they say, "It's who you know that matters."

Use the Internet

The Internet is the new frontier of job searching. Not only does it offer hundreds of places to search for job vacancies, it also provides an electronic avenue for filling out applications, sending your resume, and conducting interviews by e-mail. We hear of more and more people every day who found jobs over the Internet.

Drake Beam Morin (a New York out-placement firm) surveyed 525 unemployed people nationwide and found that 19 percent used the Internet in their job search. On average, each located five job openings—which resulted in one interview. The survey also found that job seekers under 40 had even better results. Twenty-four percent of this younger

crowd used the Internet, which resulted in seven job leads
and two interviews each.

A poll conducted by AT&T found that 80 percent of
college students in America today have free access to the
Internet, and a high percentage of those students plan to take
advantage of this access to conduct an electronic job search.
In our own survey, 20 percent of those teacher applicants
who participated said they surfed the Net looking for vacancies.

Obviously, as more people sign onto the Net every day,
the percentages will grow. Someday soon, the Internet may
be the best place to access up-to-date job listings. If you
don't have the luxury of free Internet access, you can sign on
through one of the commercial providers (such as
CompuServe or America Online) or through a provider who
offers unlimited direct access for a flat monthly rate. Of
course, this is assuming you have a computer with ample
memory, the right kind of modem, and an available telephone
line, all of which are becoming more affordable every day.

You already know if you've spent any time surfing the
Net that whatever you're searching for is never all together in
one place. And if you're looking for teaching vacancies, you'll
find them scattered all over cyberspace. Here, however, are
some of the best places to begin your search:

✓ **A school district's web site**
This is the easiest way to stay abreast of job vacancies in your favorite districts. Call to request their
web addresses.

✓ **Newsgroups**
There are dozens of teachers' newsgroups—such as
"k12.chat.teachers" and "misc.educ."— that have
teaching vacancies intermingled with their other
postings. There are also newsgroups that only post
job vacancies, such as "misc.jobs.misc." These
newsgroups serve as compassionate support groups
for out-of-work teachers. Their message is, you're

not in this alone, and there are many others going through the same process who are glad to share what they've learned, to encourage and give helpful suggestions.

✓ **Job lists on commercial online services**
Each online service has its own system for listing job vacancies. America Online, for example, offers "Help Wanted USA" and "Career Resource Library & Employment Agency Database," plus other sources.

✓ **Bulletin Board Systems (BBSs)**
BBSs provide services through direct modem dial-up that can include "read-only" information, live chat, and e-mail.

✓ **Jobtrak**
This is a great listing of teaching vacancies if you have access to it through your college or university. It is a daily posting of jobs listed with college career centers. Most placement centers have access to Jobtrak and will either print out the listings for you or let you browse the listings online yourself.

✓ **Online Career Center (OCC)**
Many universities and colleges make OCC available to their students; it is an extensive, free listing of nationwide job listings. You can search the list by geographical area or by using keywords.

✓ **Fee-based recruitment services**
These are online recruitment and placement services that usually don't charge a fee to the job seeker. They contain thousands of jobs searchable by keywords. Two such recruitment services are Online Opportunities and Job Finders.

There are hundreds of other ways to job search on the Internet; all you need is an efficient browser, plenty of patience, and ample time.

Posting Your Resume

In addition to finding jobs on the Internet, you can post your resume and hope that the jobs find you. There are many opportunities to do this through online resume services such as "misc.job.resumes" (which is a Newsgroup), through a commercial resume service (such as The Job Company), or through the OCC.

Be aware, however, that posting your resume on the Internet is a little different than sending a full 8½" x 11" sheet of paper through the mail. A resume comes up on a computer screen that has 20 available lines (if you limit your resume to a single screen, which is a smart idea). So experts advise job hunters to condense their resumes to a 20-line screen by listing only the most valuable information.

> *Of the teacher candidates in our survey, 20 percent said they surfed the Net in their pursuit of teaching vacancies.*

Filling Out Applications by E-Mail

If your job search generates interest from a school district, you may be able to fill out your application and send it by e-mail. Once your application is received, you might receive a telephone call—or you might be interviewed by e-mail as well. The ultimate goal, of course, is to receive an invitation to interview in person. E-mail applications and interviews are more common when you are searching for a job in another state or overseas.

If you're a "newbie" to cyberspace, then everything we've written here might just as well have been in a foreign language. You need to locate a good book on browsing the Internet and, more specifically, on searching for a job online.

One of the best is titled *Using the Internet and the World Wide Web in Your Job Search,* by Fred Jandt and Mary Nemnich.[1]

Once you get online, you'll be hooked. There's so much valuable information out there and more is coming online every day.

Notes

1. *Using the Internet and the World Wide Web in Your Job Search* by Fred E. Jandt and Mary B. Nemnich (Indianapolis: JIST Works, 1997).

4

Finding the Inside Track

There are several ways to find the "inside track." You can impress key people on a school's campus as you student teach, work as a volunteer, serve as a substitute or fill a temporary teaching vacancy. If you do an outstanding job in any of these positions, you're sure to be noticed by the principal, your master teacher, and others who have hiring authority or can recommend you to those who do. Don't pass up a chance to showcase yourself!

Become an Enthusiastic Student Teacher

Your student teaching experience is an important part of your job search: The evaluations from your university supervisor, master teacher, school site principal, and others are the most important references you'll have in your college placement file, because they are from professional educators who have seen your performance in the classroom or have been closely associated with it. These are the people who have evaluated your lessons, classroom management skills, and everything you've been trained to do over the last few years. These people, for now, hold your professional life in their hands—you'd better do your best to impress them!

If you are already a credentialed teacher who has completed your student teaching, you don't need to be reminded of the importance of a good, solid student teaching performance that results in great evaluations and letters of reference. But if you have your student teaching ahead of you, or if you are in the middle of it right now, you should try to impress *anyone* in a position to write letters of reference for your placement file.

> *Of the newly hired teachers in our survey, 6 percent were hired at the schools where they did their student teaching.*

You may not be particularly interested in staying in the district where you are student teaching, but the impressions you make there will follow you wherever you go. And if you *are* interested in the district where you're doing your student teaching, keep in mind that if they like you they will not want to lose you to another district! As we researched this book, that fact was made abundantly clear—and it makes sense. After all, the administrators in that district *know* you; they've seen what you can bring to their schools and to their kids. So if you make a positive impression on those folks mentioned above, they're going to want you somewhere in their district. It's a win-win deal!

In most student teaching situations, you are given a prescribed schedule to follow. For instance, in your first week or so you'll probably observe your master teacher and get to know the students in the class—and all their names. You will gradually take on more teaching responsibilities until you "go solo," when you take over the class by yourself and your master teacher stays behind the scenes as much as possible. Then, toward the end of your assignment, the master teacher will ease back into the teaching scene to smooth the transition when your solo stint is over.

Here is some helpful advice as you begin your student teaching experience: From the very start, even during the observation period, suggest interesting and creative things you can do to help your master teacher. For example, you might suggest such things as constructing a bulletin board, handling the attendance duties, or taking lunch count. Also, think of any skills you have that are teaching-related. (Remember the transferable skills we talked about in chapter 1?) These will help you develop a relationship with the kids, as well as showcase something special you can bring to the classroom.

If you are artistically talented, for example, you can add something to the room environment. If you play the guitar, think of a fun song you can teach the class. If the students are older and think it's not cool to sing "Puff the Magic Dragon," think of another, more age-appropriate song. The point is this: If you follow your prescribed student teaching schedule to the letter and never offer anything special, you're missing an opportunity to showcase yourself and begin the process of "selling your product," even at this early stage.

Another good idea is to create a network with other student teachers at your school, sharing information and getting to know them well. This can really pay off when you're further along in your job search. (We'll talk more about this valuable idea in chapter 5.)

Don't limit your networking to your fellow student teachers, however. The principal, assistant principal, and mentor teachers all can help you land that plum teaching job. And never underestimate the power and influence of school secretaries—you can take it to the bank that they know what's going on! Definitely befriend them.

Your network should include the full-time teachers at the school, as well. They often know influential people within the district. You never know, one of them may even be a close friend, a spouse, or related to someone in the district with hiring authority. We heard from several student teachers and substitute teachers in our survey who took advantage of these contacts to land great teaching positions.

So take your student teaching experience seriously. Plan on putting in long days and going the extra mile. Be in the classroom early, and be there every school day. Take advantage of every opportunity to teach and interact with students. Be dedicated; be enthusiastic.

The most important letter of reference you will have in your placement file is the one from your master teacher. After all, that person has worked more closely with you on a daily basis than anyone else. Make it easy for him or her to write an excellent letter.

Here are two examples of what your master teacher might say:

> *"You should have outstanding recommendations, so work hard at whatever you do, and go above and beyond while you're a student teacher."*
> —Member of an interview committee in Miami, Florida

"Cliff Johnson was a student teacher in my classroom during the spring semester of 1997. His attendance was satisfactory and he was usually punctual. He maintained adequate classroom control. His lessons indicated planning. . . ."

Or:

"Cliff Johnson was a student teacher in my classroom during the spring semester of 1997. He arrived early and stayed late each and every school day. His classroom control was excellent. He enthusiastically presented well-prepared lessons. . . ."

If you were screening applications and ran across these two letters, which would impress you the most? The answer is obvious. We cannot overemphasize the importance of your student teaching experience and its impact on your job search.

If you do a good job, people will hear about you. Principals talk to other principals, teachers to teachers, parents to
parents. It's like the pebble in the pond and its concentric
waves. Never underestimate the role of chance in getting a
job. Think of all the people you know who got their jobs in
some strange way: "So and so" knew "so and so" who heard
from "so and so" about a job over in Pikeville. You might say
the more "so and sos" who know you, the better chance you
have of getting a job.

Become an Enthusiastic School Volunteer

Doing volunteer work at a school is another way to make
yourself known. If you have something to offer young people
in the classroom, it will show up when you volunteer to help
out at a school; and the more exposure you get within the
educational community, the better your chances to become
known by those with hiring authority.

For starters, think about joining the school's parent-
teacher organization. Not only will you get to know the
school's principal and teachers, but they will recognize your
commitment to kids and to education. They will also get a
sense of your attitude and work ethic.

As a classroom volunteer as well, there are many ways to
impress a particular teacher as you showcase your skills,
talents, and love of children. For example, if you accompany
the class on a field trip and help the teacher cope with the
inevitable mini-crises that happen along the way, you will
create a positive impression; and you can count on your
excellent reputation filtering back to the principal and other
teachers at the school.

At the secondary level, take whatever special talents you
have—whether in drama, music, athletics, foreign languages,
or fund-raising—and volunteer to use them in some way. You
might volunteer as a chaperone for school dances. Or you
might work with a class on their yearbook, coordinate home-

coming activities, or help plan the decorations for the junior-senior prom. There are dozens of ways to help out—it just takes some creative thinking.

By offering your services as a school volunteer, not only will you be helping the kids and the staff, you'll be putting yourself on the inside track to teaching vacancies as they come up—and that's the bottom line. Look at it this way: School volunteerism is just one more way to keep your "net working." After all, the more territory your net covers, the more you make yourself known—and, as we've already learned, the first rule of the job search is to *become known!*

Become an Enthusiastic Sub or Temp

Of the newly hired teachers in our survey, 13 percent were hired for full-time positions at the schools where they had worked as substitute teachers.

As we researched this book, we talked to many teachers who were hired by the school or district where they had worked as substitute teachers. Some had subbed on a day-to-day basis, others had filled part-time or temporary positions. If you are having trouble finding a full-time job, this may be the route for you.

Short-Term Subbing

If you decide to try subbing, it is important to be available when a school calls. And, although the telephone shouldn't dominate your life, it can certainly put a kink in your day. You may resent having to sit by the phone certain times of the day waiting for that call.

Usually you will be called before 7 A.M. Someone from the school or the sub service will ask if you're available to take a certain class for that day. You always have the option to decline, of course, and on occasion you will have to, for any number of reasons. But if you want to maintain a good working relationship with a district, don't make a habit of turning them down. If you do, they will stop calling. Of course, if you're signed up to sub with several districts, there will be times you are forced to decline one job because you have already taken another, which is one of the disadvantages of spreading yourself too thin.

When you do get called to fill in as a sub, do a good job. Be on time, and be prepared. Treat the class as if it were your own, maintain control—and don't let the students run all over you. Try to accomplish all the regular teacher's lesson plans for the day, and leave detailed notes and comments on your progress. Keep these comments as upbeat and positive as possible, but don't be afraid to let the teacher know about any students who misbehaved.

You need to realize that the teacher/substitute relationship is a symbiotic one. The teacher depends on you to carry out the plans prepared for that day's lessons. But you, as a substitute teacher in the midst of a job hunt, are actually more dependent on the teacher than the teacher is on you. After all, the teacher already has a full-time job, and you don't. The point is this: It's important for you to impress the teacher by doing a superior job of subbing.

If you develop a reputation for doing your best to carry out the teacher's lesson plans, taking time to jot down notes, and maintaining good control of the classroom, this reputation spreads fast around the district. Having such a reputation certainly gives you a leg up on your competition when it comes to landing a full-time job.

Note: Several excellent books on substitute teaching are available at your local teacher supply store. These are usually inexpensive and very helpful for the beginning substitute teacher.

When you serve as a short- or long-term substitute teacher, you become *known* in the school and the district, and becoming *known* is the number one goal of all job seekers, regardless of the profession. Many teacher-candidates sign up to sub in several different districts, in fact, multiplying their chances to become known for their teaching skills, their ability to get along with parents and staff, and their enthusiasm and flexibility. Often, these substitutes get called to one school or another every day of the week.

Long-Term Subbing

If you agree to take on a temporary position (also known as long-term subbing) you have an even better chance to shine, impressing your fellow teachers, the secretaries, mentor teachers, and administrators over a longer period of time. Many teachers seek out temporary positions for this very reason, especially if the school or district is one where they would be happy in a full-time position.

"Long-term substitute positions are valuable, and networking with teachers in buildings in which I subbed led me to references I might not otherwise have had."
—*11th-grade history teacher in New Jersey*

What many teacher-candidates don't realize is that those who accept temporary positions often are placed in a hiring pool for full-time positions that become available in the future. In fact, one administrator in the San Francisco Bay area told us that *all* new teaching positions are offered first to those in the temporary and part-time hiring pool from the previous year. We also heard of several cases in which teachers had to leave the classroom for personal or health reasons and were unable to return. The substitutes who took over and did good jobs in those situations had the inside track when the job vacancies were officially advertised.

As long-time teachers and administrators, we can vouch for the fact that short- and long-term subbing often leads to a full-time position. It is, in fact, a great method to get yourself *known* and eventually hired.

Think of your subbing experience as another way to extend your network every time you are called to a new school. Any teacher, principal, or secretary you impress with your attitude and professionalism could be your pipeline to that ideal teaching position.

Be patient and persistent. And if you choose substitute teaching as a bridge to your own full-time position, just remember that subbing will make you that much better prepared for the exciting day you walk into your very own classroom. And you will—it's coming soon!

5

Preparing for the Interview

The first step in preparing for an interview is knowing as much as you can about the schools and the surrounding community where you are interviewing. This knowledge serves two purposes: It helps you determine if you really want to work in a given school or community, and it puts you at an advantage during the interview itself.

These are important considerations. The former can keep you from accepting a job you will hate. The latter gives you an edge over other candidates. Interview committees are favorably impressed by candidates who take the time to research their schools and communities. It shows that you are willing to put in extra effort and that you are genuinely interested *in them*. Conversely, they'll know very quickly if you've just popped in and don't have a clue about them or their district.

Research the Community

There are several ways to become familiar with a community. If you can visit the prospective community, the job becomes much easier.

If the school is located in a city, try to determine its attendance area (that area from which the school draws its students). In the case of elementary schools (grades K through 6), the area probably will be smaller. Typically, urban elementary pupils live within one to two miles of their schools. A junior high school (grades 6 through 8 or 7 through 9) may serve the graduates of many elementary schools, making its attendance area much larger. Finally, a senior high (grades 9 or 10 through 12) may serve the graduates of one or two junior high schools. Sometimes, in fact, a rather large city will have only one high school.

If the school is located in a rural area, it may have a large attendance area covering many miles. In such situations there may be only one elementary school and one high school serving pupils living 10 or more miles in all directions.

Once you have determined the attendance area, drive or bicycle through it. Talk with people or students you meet. Are they friendly and helpful? Ask how youth-oriented the community is. Do they provide parks, recreational facilities, and programs for their young people? Take note of the general appearance of the community. Are the houses and yards reasonably neat and clean? If you meet someone who really impresses you, try to remember his or her name.

Spend half a day wandering around the area and you will get a good feel for the community. It will be warm, friendly, and trusting; cold, unfriendly, and suspicious; or something in between. By the end of your tour you will probably have a definite opinion about the community and its residents.

If you are unable to visit the community before the interview, you can still find out something about it by contacting the Chamber of Commerce and requesting relevant

> *Of the teacher-candidates in our survey, 49 percent said they had researched the communities where they were scheduled to be interviewed.*

information. If there is no Chamber of Commerce, try the local Visitors' Bureau or subscribe to a local newspaper for a month. While these sources won't substitute for actually being there, they can provide worthwhile information.

In chapter 3 we talked about school surveys as part of your researching. Although the research you do here is similar, there is one big difference: The school surveys were part of your job-search strategy; the research you're doing now is to prepare you for a scheduled interview for a specific position. Your motivation for researching the community takes on a new, and more exciting, meaning.

Research the School District

> *Of the teacher candidates in our survey, 21 percent tried to learn as much as possible about the policies of the school district where they were scheduled to be interviewed.*

In addition to researching the community, you should research the school district and the particular school where you will be working if you are hired.

There are many sources of information on schools and school districts.

✓ You should start with the **State Schools Directory** for your state. This resource is available in your college library or placement office and lists each county office of education for the state and the districts and schools within each county or parish, along with each school's address, telephone number, size, grades taught, and administrators.

✓ Another source is the **County Schools Directory**, which includes more detailed information, such as each school's staff and grade assignments.

✓ Finally, the most comprehensive source of information on a particular school is the **school's directory** or handbook, which is available at the school itself.

When you've gathered all these resources, you'll have the information you need for a given school or district.

Some states require their schools to provide a "school report card" to their state education department. These documents contain a brief description of the school, including its location, the community it serves, its size, grades taught, and ethnicity.

Here are some other items often included in a school report card:

✓ Student attendance
✓ Amount of money spent per student
✓ Type of textbooks used
✓ Salary information
✓ Current training and curriculum projects
✓ Leadership provided
✓ Results of student achievement tests
✓ Description of the facilities
✓ Classroom discipline and climate for learning
✓ Teacher evaluation policy
✓ Student support services offered

These reports provide useful information for comparing one school with another.

Visit the School

Finally, the ultimate school research opportunity is a visit to an individual school campus. Most administrators welcome nonintrusive visits from teacher-candidates. Notice we said "nonintrusive." Keep in mind the school's primary function is to educate students, and your visit should interfere as little as possible with that function.

Call the school in advance and explain why you'd like to visit. Your evaluation of the school begins with this phone call. Chances are you will talk with the school secretary—usually a school's "initial image." How were you received? How efficiently did the person deal with your request?

Assuming you're given permission to visit, be sure to show up on time. You should dress appropriately—as if you were coming for an interview. No shorts and tank tops; no scuffed tennis shoes *sans* socks. You get the idea.

> *"Interviewers appreciate an interviewee who is prepared."*
> —Max Eggert in The Perfect Interview

As you drive up to the campus, check out its general appearance. Are the grounds free of litter? Does the landscaping look good?

Next, check out the building itself. Is the paint in good condition? Is there litter or graffiti? Are the windows and doors clean? The age of the building shouldn't affect the learning going on inside its walls; in fact, an old building that's clean and well-maintained will almost always house an educational program superior to that of a newer building that's dirty and poorly maintained. The physical appearance of a school tells volumes about its students, staff, and program.

As you enter the building, what do you see? Are signs posted giving clear directions to the office, or are you greeted with blank walls and left to figure it out for yourself? Go to the office immediately, by the way, because administrators don't like strangers wandering around the campus.

As you enter the office, are you met with a warm greeting and a smile? Or do you feel like you're entering a war zone? Do you sense a cold, "What do you want, can't you see we're busy here?" attitude? In most cases, you will be received with a warm greeting. School secretaries, we've found, are almost always friendly and helpful.

At this time you will be given directions for your visit. You may have an opportunity to visit briefly with the principal, or the secretary may direct you to a particular classroom. If you visit a classroom, the general rule is to enter without knocking. If the teacher is presenting a lesson or working with a group of students, move to the back of the room and wait for the teacher to come to you. If the teacher is not occupied with students when you enter, approach him or her and introduce yourself. The teacher will then tell you where to sit during your observation. It's usually best to observe from the rear of the classroom so you don't distract the students.

> *"Talking to teachers in the district (where I was to be interviewed) got me headed in the right direction."*
>
> *—Middle-grade science teacher in North Dakota*

Try to talk with any staff members you meet during your visit; they will help you form an opinion of the school. Visit the playground and the staff room during breaks and the student dining area and faculty lounge during lunch.

If you spend only three hours on a campus (say, from 10 A.M. to 1 P.M.), you won't know everything about a school, but you'll know considerably more than most candidates for the position.

Before leaving the campus check back at the office and thank those responsible for your visit. You might also send a thank-you note later that day. This is a classy touch that makes you stand out from other candidates.

Taking time to research a community and its schools won't assure you a job; however, it will enhance your chances of being offered a contract—and it just may keep you from signing a contract you would regret later.

Network with Other Teacher-Candidates

In chapter 3, we discussed networking as a process of making contacts and establishing relationships as part of the job search. The kind of networking we're talking about here is the same concept, but on a much smaller scale. It involves forming a network of a half-dozen or so of your teacher-candidate friends. This cozy little group, in effect, becomes a support group as much as a networking team, so it's important to find people who share some basic qualities with you, including these:

✓ They have a sense of humor
✓ They are seeking jobs close to the same grade level
✓ They share common ideas about the job search
✓ They buy into the philosophy of small-group net-working

Although it's best to have at least five or six members, if you can find only three or four who meet the criteria, go ahead and form a group. The group's closeness and compatibility are more important than the number of members.

Here are some ways you and the members of your network group can be helpful to one another:

Of those responding to our survey, 52 percent said they networked with other teacher-candidates, sharing tips and lending support.

✓ You can share ideas and information about job leads and job search tips.
✓ You give and receive advice and constructive criticism. (Remember, this should always be done in a good spirit.)
✓ You encourage each other as much as possible.
✓ You can do mock interviews and role playing, and respond to hypotheticals and possible

interview questions (more about these later in this chapter).

✓ You discuss strategies of the interview process, like these:
- Questions that should be asked during the interview
- Questions to be avoided during the interview
- Body language
- Social skills
- Voice, grooming, and attire
- Attitude

As members of the group sign teaching contracts, they should be encouraged to stay with the group as long as they can, offering support, encouragement, and constructive criticism, especially during mock interviews.

"Networking with other teacher candidates led me to pursue job openings of which I was originally unaware."
—Secondary social studies teacher in New Jersey

One note of caution regarding these networking groups: Remember that your small support group is only one part of your total networking effort. Don't let your cozy little group become so warm and comfortable that you neglect your other job search efforts.

Later, we'll talk about a couple ways to put your group to work, specifically as you prepare for the interview itself. You'll find suggestions for using a video camera during your meetings, which will boost your confidence when it comes time for real interviews. You'll also see why we listed "a sense of humor" as an absolute necessity for each member of the group.

It should be fun, so read on.

Prepare Responses to Possible Interview Questions

When you walk into an interview room, you will have about 30 minutes to sell yourself. During this brief time you may be asked only 8 or 10 questions. Your responses to these questions are crucial. Because you don't know which questions will be asked, you need to be prepared.

The fact that you were called for an interview—that you made the paper cut—means they like you so far. Now it's up to you to impress them with your excellent responses to their questions. Your responses should be clear and concise; don't ramble on and on. Make your point and go on! If you're asked a straightforward question, give a straightforward answer. On the other hand, if you're asked an open-ended question, always take it as a valuable opportunity to tell the interview panel what you want them to know. This may be a good time to work in some of your special skills and talents or to share something from your portfolio. Sell yourself!

As we gathered information for this book, we asked interviewers what questions they typically ask at the interview table. We also asked newly hired teachers what questions they were asked during their interviews. We combined these two lists, discarded any questions that related to isolated situations, and grouped the remaining questions into two categories: **The Top 20 Questions Asked During Interviews** and **Other Frequently Asked Questions.**

The Top 20 Questions Asked During Interviews

Be prepared to respond to these questions, because you will undoubtedly hear many of them during your interviews. Practice your responses with a friend or in front of your networking group. Ask for their constructive criticism of your answers, then polish your performance until you can respond in a natural way without hesitation.

We have given you some help on this priority list of questions by offering comments about *What They're Really Asking* and *Tips* to help you prepare.

1. **What is your greatest strength as a teacher?**

    What they're really asking:
    - ✓ How do you perceive your talents and abilities as a teacher?
    - ✓ Will you be an asset to our school and our students?

    Tips:
    - ✓ They're crying for you to sell yourself here; don't let them down.
    - ✓ Have 6 or 7 responses written and ready on a 3" x 5" card.
    - ✓ Don't blow smoke.
    - ✓ Be "confidently humble."

2. **What is your greatest weakness?**

    What they're really asking:
    - ✓ How honest are you being with us and with yourself?
    - ✓ How realistic are you?
    - ✓ What skeletons do you have in your "teaching closet" that we should know about?

    Tips:
    - ✓ Review the section in chapter 1 on ways to present a weakness as a positive.
    - ✓ Don't sell yourself down the river with your response.

3. **What can you tell us about yourself?**

    What they're really asking:
    - ✓ What makes you special?
    - ✓ Why should we hire you?
    - ✓ How organized and concise are you?
    - ✓ How confident are you?
    - ✓ What might you bring to our children?
    - ✓ Who are you? Do we want you to work with our children?

Tips:

- ✓ Use most of your response time selling yourself.
- ✓ Have several powerful selling points ready for this one.
- ✓ Give a brief, concise response in less than two minutes.
- ✓ This is an open-ended question, a chance for you to impress them.
- ✓ This is no time for humility, but don't step over the line of arrogance either.

4. What is your philosophy of classroom discipline?

What they're really asking:

- ✓ Do you *have* a plan?
- ✓ How will you implement your plan?
- ✓ Do you think this is important?
- ✓ Are you going to be able to control kids?

Tips:

- ✓ Be ready to give an example of a discipline "ladder" or plan.
- ✓ Be prepared to tell why you like it, and give examples of how it's worked for you.
- ✓ Discipline is one of the most important areas of concern in schools today. Handle this subject well!

5. What steps would you take with a student who is disruptive in your classroom?

What they're really asking:

- ✓ Do you have a classroom discipline plan?
- ✓ Can you handle most discipline problems yourself, or will you send students to the principal's office at the drop of a hat?
- ✓ What is your general philosophy of classroom discipline?

Tips:

- ✓ This question is similar to question 4; be ready to describe a discipline plan and how you plan to implement it.
- ✓ Reaffirm your philosophy of discipline.

✓ Again, the subject of classroom discipline is a major concern for most hiring panels.

6. **What kind of classroom management plan do you like best? How would you implement it in your classroom?**

   What they're really asking:
   ✓ If we walk into your classroom, what will we see going on?
   ✓ How will your lessons be planned?
   ✓ Will your students be on task and challenged?

   Tips:
   ✓ You need to explain your management plan briefly, completely, and in an organized way.
   ✓ Interview committees are not looking for a morgue setting; nor do they want the center ring of a three-ring circus. They are looking for an intellectually stimulating, organized, respectful environment in which students do well academically and socially.
   ✓ Explain how you will implement your plan in terms of behavior; recall your teacher education classes and your student teaching experiences.
   ✓ You will almost certainly be asked a question similar to this because it is a critical area of importance in most school districts.

7. **Why do you want to be a teacher?**

   What they're really asking:
   ✓ How dedicated are you?
   ✓ Do you have a passion for children and the teaching profession?
   ✓ How will our children benefit by having you as their teacher?

   Tips:
   ✓ If you have a passion for kids, this one should be easy. Don't get carried away though, keep it simple and to the point.

✓ Stay away from a response like, "Most of my family members have been teachers." This won't get you very far.

8. **Why do you want to teach in this district/school?**
What they're really asking:
   ✓ Do you care where you teach?
   ✓ Did you take the time to research our district/school?
   ✓ Are you right for our schools and our children?
Tips:
   ✓ This is a great PR question. If your school survey showed this district to be high on your list, the answer will come easily. Without overdoing it, tell them how great they are!
   ✓ Tell them that you *do* want to work for them!

9. **Why should we hire you for this position?**
What they're really asking:
   ✓ Can you convince us that you're the one?
   ✓ Can you sell your "product?"
   ✓ How much confidence do you have in yourself?
Tips:
   ✓ Be ready to make a powerful statement of your value to the school or district.
   ✓ This is no time for humility, but don't be arrogant either.

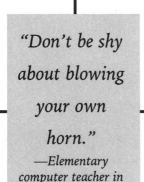

"Don't be shy about blowing your own horn."
—Elementary computer teacher in Massachusetts

10. **What are your goals in education? Where do you see yourself five years from now? How does this position fit into your career plans?**

What they're really asking:
   ✓ Do you want to stay in one position for the long haul, or will you be here a year and move on?

✓ Are you a stable person?

✓ Have you set goals for yourself?

✓ Have you given any thought to your future?

Tips:

✓ They want another perspective on you.

✓ They might not want to hire someone who will be moving down the road in a year or two.

✓ There's nothing wrong with simply saying that you have one goal in mind right now, and that is to become the best teacher possible.

11. **What would we see if we walked into your classroom?**

What they're really asking:

✓ What is your philosophy of education?

✓ What kind of a teacher are you?

✓ Do you have a well-managed classroom?

✓ Are your students interacting with you and the other students?

Tips:

✓ This is a good time for name dropping. Show off your knowledge of new and proven methods and trends (e.g., grouping of students, Cooperative Learning, and use of manipulatives and hands-on teaching materials).

✓ You might say: "You would see the students arranged in groups; a pleasant atmosphere; a room that is comfortable and pleasing to the eye; students who are under control, yet busy with a healthy amount of noise going on; children learning in different modalities: visual, auditory, and kinesthetic."

✓ Avoid the tendency to go into too much detail. They might be interested in the way you will arrange the students' desks, but they don't really want to know what's inside each desk.

12. **What are some trends, issues, and methodologies in education that relate to your specific curriculum area or grade level?**

What they're really asking:
- ✓ Do you know what's going on in education today?
- ✓ Do you have a passion for the profession of teaching?

Tips:
- ✓ Read educational journals and periodicals regularly.
- ✓ Familiarize yourself with current trends and buzz words in education.
- ✓ Talk with your peers and other educators in your field.
- ✓ Visit schools as often as you can to observe the latest teaching methods.
- ✓ Join a professional organization.

13. **What book are you currently reading or have you read recently?**

What they're really asking:
- ✓ Teachers should be avid readers; are you a reader?
- ✓ What are your interests?
- ✓ How well-rounded are you?

Tips:
- ✓ This question is often asked, so be ready for it.
- ✓ If you've lost the recreational reading "bug" because of your hectic schedule, take some time to read a variety of fiction, nonfiction, and professional books.

14. **What are some of your hobbies or leisure-time activities?**

What they're really asking:
- ✓ How well-rounded are you?
- ✓ What do you do outside of school that would transfer positively into the classroom?

Tips:

✓ Here's another opportunity to sell yourself; take advantage of questions like these.

✓ Emphasize any of your hobbies or leisure-time activities that could carry over to your classroom.

✓ The interview committee is trying to find out more about you, and they know your life outside the classroom can tell them a lot. So don't just *answer* questions; *respond* to them.

15. **What special skills or talents will you bring to your classroom?**

What they're really asking:

✓ How well-rounded are you?

✓ Do you have a wide variety of interests and experiences that will make you an exciting, stimulating teacher?

Tips:

✓ Yes! Your time to shine.

✓ Be prepared to state in an organized, succinct fashion any skills or talents you will bring to their school, but be careful you don't overdo it.

16. **Would you be willing to teach at a different grade level (elementary) or teach a different subject (secondary)?**

What they're really asking:

✓ Are you flexible?

✓ Do you have enough confidence to consider other grade levels or subject areas?

✓ How's your attitude?

Tips:

✓ You need to think about this possibility in advance. The committee may have already found the right person for the advertised position, and now they're looking for someone who can adapt to their needs if another position becomes available. Administrators like to have options, and they are always looking for teachers who are flexible and versatile.

✓ A positive response here might give you a leg up on your competition!

17. **Would you be willing to pursue an extra certificate or credential?**

   What they're really asking:
   - ✓ How is your attitude?
   - ✓ How flexible are you?
   - ✓ Are you a teacher who will increase our staffing options?

   Tips:
   - ✓ School districts are frequently required to employ teachers who have special credentials or certificates in order to qualify for special program funds. If you have certain specialized credentials or certificates in addition to your basic teaching credential, you become more valuable to the district.
   - ✓ If all things are equal, the position will go to the candidate who is willing to pursue one of these "extras."
   - ✓ This is a perfect time to tell the hiring panel "how important professional growth is to me."

18. **What is your philosophy of team teaching?**

   What they're really asking:
   - ✓ Are you flexible?
   - ✓ Do you work well with others?
   - ✓ Do you have experience in team teaching?
   - ✓ Do you know anything about the methodology of team teaching?

   Tips:
   - ✓ Be prepared to talk about this concept in a favorable way.
   - ✓ Share a few positive points in favor of team teaching, such as these:
     - Team teaching is a powerful and efficient method for dealing with a large number of students.

- It is very effective for teachers to work together and share their ideas.
- You might say, "I haven't had the opportunity to be involved in a teaming situation yet, but I understand it can offer a more efficient use of time in the classroom." Or, "If teachers at my grade level have determined that team teaching would better the learning process of our students, I'm very willing to try it. I enjoy working and sharing with other teachers, and I want the best for our kids."

19. **What were you hoping we would ask you today, but didn't?**

What they're really asking:
   ✓ Is there anything special about yourself you want us to know?

Tips:
   ✓ Speak up—sell yourself.
   ✓ This is a great opportunity to "show and tell" one more time, using materials from your portfolio to convince them how valuable you will be to their district. Go for it!

20. **Do you have any questions for us?**

What they're really asking:
   ✓ Are you interested enough in our district to ask questions?
   ✓ How prepared are you to ask questions?
   ✓ Have you given this some thought?

Tips:
   ✓ See "Questions You Should Ask" in chapter 7.
   ✓ Be sure you have at least one question ready to ask, or have five or six listed on a 3" x 5" card. The panel will be impressed that you came prepared.
   ✓ *Never* say, "No, you've answered all my questions."

Other Frequently Asked Questions

Read through this list of questions and decide how you will respond to each one. Ask yourself, "What are they really asking?" This will help you prepare.

> "Have opinions about current educational issues because they will come up in the interview."
>
> —K-12 P.E. teacher in Charlottesville, Virginia

21. At what point do you involve the principal in a discipline matter?

22. What is your description of an ideal teacher?

23. What are your plans for professional growth?

24. If you were hired to teach starting this September, how would you go about setting up your reading program?

25. Do you prefer homogeneous or heterogeneous grouping? Why?

26. In which curriculum areas do you feel particularly strong?

27. Would you be willing to coach a sport, advise an organization, or assist with extracurricular activities?

28. What experience do you have with this age group?

29. Do you see yourself as a "team player?"

30. How would you motivate a student who won't even try?

31. Describe a time when a lesson was not going well; what did you do about it?

32. How would you compare the Whole Language approach to reading to a Phonics-Based approach?

33. How would you implement Cooperative Grouping in your classroom?

34. What are some ways you would communicate with a parent regarding a student's progress?

35. While in high school and college, in which extracurricular activities did you participate? Did you hold an office?

36. How would you integrate language arts across the curriculum?

37. What community projects or organizations have you been involved with?

38. How would your best friend describe you?

39. How do you spend your spare time?

40. Who are some people who have had a great impact on your life?

> *"The most important thing is that teacher-candidates really know their subject areas."*
>
> —*Member of panel that interviews teachers on the secondary level in Florida*

41. What would you like to share about your student teaching experience?

42. What do you think are the critical skills required to be a successful teacher?

43. Do you involve parents in your classroom?

44. What kind of principal would you like to work for?

45. What do you know about our school district?

46. How do you go about deciding what should be taught in your classroom?

47. What provides you the greatest pleasure in teaching?

48. What is your philosophy and practice of the teacher's role as a "member of the school staff?"

49. How would you go about grouping your students in mathematics?

50. What does Individualized Instruction mean to you?

> *"During the interview be confident, relaxed, professional, knowledgeable, and willing to work as part of a team."*
>
> *—Music teacher and department chair for small school district in Washington*

51. Which evaluation techniques or testing procedures would you use to determine student academic growth?

52. How effective is it to call parents for a conference when a problem has developed with their son or daughter?

53. Describe a belief you hold about education. How would you implement it in the classroom?

54. What are some of the new teaching textbooks and materials being used in your grade level or in your subject area?

55. What is your philosophy regarding the Thematic Approach in teaching the curriculum?

56. At which grade level do you feel you would do the best job?

57. Have you had any background in designing lesson plans with Behavioral Objectives in your teaching? How do you feel about them?

58. Are there any undesirable things you can think of about teaching?

59. What is the worst thing that ever happened to you in the classroom?

60. Do you feel your job as a teacher goes beyond the three o'clock bell? How?

61. How much time, if any, would you be able to spend working on after-school projects or programs?

62. What should the job of principal entail?

63. How would you handle varied reading abilities in the content areas?

64. An experienced teacher offers you the following advice: "When you are teaching, be sure to command the respect of your students immediately and everything will go well." How do you feel about this?

65. How will you go about determining your students' attitudes and feelings toward your class?

66. What would you say to a parent who complains that your teaching is irrelevant to his or her child's needs?

67. What would you do with a student who is obviously gifted or talented in a particular area?

68. What are some ways a student can show mastery of a concept?

69. What is meant by Diagnostic and Prescriptive Learning?

70. What are Negative Consequences and Positive Reinforcement, and the effects of each?

71. What steps would you take to turn a habitually tardy student into a punctual student?

72. How do you motivate students to develop self-discipline?

73. What are some ways to let parents know about the positive things going on in your classroom?

74. What would you tell a parent who complains that you don't give his or her child enough homework?

75. If we asked your closest teaching associate to tell us how well you get along with children and adults, what would that person say?

76. How did you happen to choose your college major?

77. What kind of relationship should teachers develop with their students?

> *"This is not the time to be tongue-tied. Decide what you can bring to the job and try to communicate that in your interview."*
> —An elementary school health and P.E. teacher in Charlottesville, Virginia

78. How would you establish and maintain positive relationships with students, parents, staff, and others in the community?

79. Briefly describe your philosophy and practice of the teacher's role as a Director of Learning.

80. What do you understand the Inquiry Method to be in the areas of science and social science?

81. What is your attitude toward Individual versus Total Class discipline?

82. If you started teaching in the middle of the school year, how would you get to know the students and their parents?

83. What do you think is wrong with education today? What is right?

84. If another teacher is habitually late relieving you on yard duty, what would you do?

85. What do you believe is the major purpose of a teacher's evaluation by a principal?

86. What are some personality characteristics you find unbearable in people?

87. If students constantly complained to you about another teacher, what would you do?

88. If we were to contact your current supervisor or evaluator about your student teaching performance, what would that person say?

89. What professional association meetings have you attended within the past year?

90. How would you teach Critical Thinking to your students?

91. How would you use Authentic Assessment?

Here are a few final words of advice:
- ✓ Don't let your responses sound "canned" or rehearsed; pause before responding to a question, as if giving it serious thought.
- ✓ Keep your best skills and traits in mind as you respond to questions; be ready to work them into the dialogue in a natural way.
- ✓ If you're a new teacher and can't respond to some of the panel's questions based on past classroom experience, emphasize your many job-related skills that can be transferred to the classroom. Also let the panel see your enthusiasm, motivation, and passion for children and for the teaching profession.

A Word About Coaching

Many teacher-candidates in our survey reported being asked if they would be willing to coach a sport in addition to teaching their regular classes. Coaching isn't for everyone, obviously, but if you have an interest in athletics in general, or in one sport in particular, you should definitely consider pursuing this "extra" for these reasons:

> *"Be willing to coach, volunteer for academic games and clubs. I got my job because I was willing to coach football and track. It's hard to find good people to do these things."*
>
> —*Secondary science teacher in Michigan*

✓ If the district needs someone to coach a sport in addition to teaching a regular single-subject curriculum, this could very well land you the position. This is especially true in smaller schools.

✓ You would ordinarily be compensated for your coaching. An extra $800 to $1,500 each year could be very attractive.

✓ Coaching can create special contacts with kids. Most coaches would agree that the coach/athlete relationship can be powerful and make a life-long, positive impact on a young person's life. Stepping out of your role in the classroom and onto the playing field can break down barriers that inhibit a child's trust of you.

✓ Coaching can be, and often is, a lot of fun. We have spent many hours after school in the gym or on the playing field. If you're considering coaching as one more way to market yourself, don't overlook the "fun factor."

Rehearse Role-Playing and Hypotheticals

Thirty-eight percent of the teacher candidates in our survey were asked to role-play or respond to hypotheticals during their interviews; only 20 percent of them had prepared for it ahead of time.

First, let's look at the difference between role-playing and hypotheticals. In dealing with a hypothetical, you must explain how you would handle a given scenario the panel has set up for you. Here is an example: "How would you deal with an angry parent who comes into your classroom during a class session and demands your immediate attention?"

In role-playing, you assume the role of the teacher and the interview panel plays the "devil's advocate," such as a group of parents who want to confront you over a particular issue. For example, you, as the teacher, must defend your position on Whole Language versus Phonics-Based reading. The hiring panel will take the position of the parent group who opposes your view. This is play-acting, and it takes most of us out of our comfort zone in a heartbeat. For this reason, it is important to rehearse role-playing with your friends. Our survey shows that it's not often required during an interview, but it does happen, so you need to be prepared.

As you practice role-playing and responding to hypotheticals, you need to picture possible interview settings. One setting would be a one-on-one interview in which the principal sits behind a desk and you sit directly in front of it. If an interview panel is conducting the interview, panel members usually sit at a large table and you sit at a desk or smaller table 10 to 15 feet in front of them.

The atmosphere of the interview can be formal or informal, depending on the administrator or the makeup of the interview team. Most interviewers try to promote a relaxed atmosphere in the hope that you will feel free to be yourself so they can see the "real you."

> *Of the teacher-candidates in our survey, 38 percent reported being asked to role-play or respond to hypotheticals during an interview, but only 20 percent of them had rehearsed ahead of time.*

It's natural to be a little nervous during an interview, but to this we say, "Trust us." We can't think of a single interview we've been involved in that was an unpleasant experience. So as you prepare for your interviews, remember to relax, be yourself, and enjoy the experience. Try to have a positive mind-set as you practice role-playing and responding to hypotheticals.

Here are some of the most common hypotheticals presented during interviews. You would be asked to respond to each scenario:

✓ One of your students becomes disruptive
✓ A student reveals some very personal concerns, then withdraws and says nothing further
✓ One of your students becomes violent
✓ A parent becomes very angry during a parent-teacher conference
✓ One of your students doesn't respond to your discipline plan
✓ Take a position on Whole Language or Phonics and defend it
✓ You suspect a project turned in by a student was completed by someone else
✓ After you've given an assignment, you notice a student quietly crying
✓ Two of your students are fighting
✓ A student refuses to salute the flag or observe certain holidays
✓ You observe a student cheating on a test during class

✓ A student reveals a situation at home that makes you think she may be the victim of some kind of abuse

✓ You disagree with your principal's method of handling a given situation

✓ One of your students becomes belligerent and defies you

✓ A student brings you some money, says he found it, then wants to know if he can have it later to keep

✓ You feel your principal is not supporting you in a difficult situation

✓ A student has an accident on the playground; he is on the ground and unable to move

This is by no means a complete list of the scenarios you may encounter during an interview. One thing you can count on, however, is that a significant number of scenarios will involve either a confrontational situation with a parent or a discipline/behavior problem with a student.

It's obvious that school districts place a tremendous emphasis on discipline and classroom management. And you only have to read the newspapers to see why. They want to feel confident that you, as a new teacher, have a good, sound, fair method of class management; you can't wimp out in this area. So, before you go into the interview, be sure you have a specific discipline plan in mind. Review what you learned in your teacher training courses and from your reading. You also may want to consider the solid, practical ideas in our first book, *The Unauthorized Teacher's Survival Guide*. In chapter 7 of that book, we suggest many discipline methods and ideas of our own, as well as those of experts in the field.

As we discussed earlier, it's helpful to network with other teacher-candidates as you prepare for interviews. It's especially helpful to rehearse your role-playing and responses to hypotheticals with this group. Find out what scenarios have been presented during other interviews and reenact them during your networking time together.

It's also a good idea for someone in your networking group to throw in a real ringer once in a while, such as this

one, which was actually asked of one of our survey participants:

> ✓ Billie is passing around pamphlets denying the
> Holocaust. What do you do?

Wow! What *do* you do? We remember when the toughies
would be something like, "Suzie has an eraser stuck up her
nose," or "Jason threw up in the back of the bus."

If you're asked a really sticky question (like the Holo-
caust question above), you can always tell the hiring panel
that you would seek the advice of your site administrator.
And if the interview committee throws you a very difficult
hypothetical, remember that there may be several appropriate responses, and what they may *really* want to know is how
you think and react on the spot.

That's why it's so important for you to practice role-
playing and reacting to hypotheticals *before* your first interview.

Videotape Mock Interviews

Now that you've prepared your responses to interview
questions and practiced role-playing and responding to
hypotheticals, it's time to videotape a mock interview. You
will find this to be the most valuable thing you can do in
preparation for the real thing.

Get together with some of your networking buddies and
find yourselves a *very* private room where you can get down
to the serious business of videotaping one another. We know
this is an intimidating exercise for some people, but—trust
us on this one—you will be rewarded at the interview table.
Participation in mock interviews, especially if you can see
yourself on videotape, will improve your confidence level,
your use of body language, your voice level and speech patterns, and your ability to articulate responses clearly and
concisely.

Here are the ground rules:

✓ You will need one video camera, plus one videotape *per person*.

✓ Take turns being "it" while the rest of the group plays the part of the interview panel, asking questions and presenting hypothetical scenarios for you to respond to.

✓ After each candidate's performance, replay the tape and immediately participate in an open, honest, *constructive* critique. Make notes of the problem areas you want to work on before your next videotaping session.

✓ Take turns until you've all had your 15 minutes of fame.

✓ Schedule another group taping session as soon as possible, preferably within two weeks.

✓ Take your tape with you so you can watch your performance once more in the privacy of your home. Study the tape carefully and work on your flaws before the next session.

Schedule a third and final taping session to which everyone wears their interview attire. By this time you will be familiar with our tips for sharpening your personal appeal (listed in chapter 6) and be able to share some helpful advice. This final session is a good time to present a mini-lesson in front of the camera. Although only 6 percent of the teacher-candidates in our survey said they were asked to plan or present an impromptu mini-lesson during an interview, it doesn't hurt to be prepared, just in case.

Have fun with these mock interviews. Be prepared to laugh and be laughed at in a good-natured way. When we first discussed these networking groups earlier in the chapter, you may recall that a sense of humor was listed as a necessary attribute for each and every member; now you know why. There's no way to get through these mock interview sessions without cracking up at some point, but it's all part of the experience.

By the way, you may want to do two rounds of taping during the first session, one round of questions and responses followed by a round of role-playing and responding to hypotheticals. This way you won't be constantly shifting gears between the two interviewing styles.

What is the value of all this? Why suffer through such an uncomfortable exercise? Because there is no way to really know how you come across during an interview until you see yourself on videotape. This means laying your pride aside and putting your ego on the line as you watch yourself make the mistakes we all make under the pressure of a camera and in front of our peers.

Of the teacher-candidates in our survey, 6 percent said they were asked to plan or present mini-lessons during their interviews.

You may be surprised to see yourself as others see you: twirling a ring around and around on your finger as you speak; saying "you know" every other sentence; or crossing your arms in front of you when asked a question (a nonverbal sign that you resent the question or dislike the interviewer). However, by detecting these flaws ahead of time, you can make some changes: to hold your hands still; to stop saying "you know"; and to replace your negative closed position with a warm, positive, open posture.

The value of these sessions is great, although you may not realize it until you get to the interview table, where you'll feel ready for just about anything. We realize, of course, that you may be asked a few questions that are worded differently than those listed earlier. But the underlying motives for the questions will be the same, and the confidence you gain through the mock interviews will be immeasurable.

And here's a special word of encouragement for you, if you are one of those people who say, "I just don't interview well," or "I choke when I get to the interview table." You will find that by participating in these mock interviews, your fears will dissipate substantially (though they probably won't disappear altogether). Just remember that everyone who sits on a hiring panel expects to see a certain amount of nervousness at the interview table. For that matter, we've had several personnel directors, principals, and other members of interview committees tell us that *they* get nervous or uncomfortable when conducting an interview.

> *"Practice your*
>
> *interviews!"*
>
> —*A member of an interview committee for a rural school district in Idaho*

So, don't let the butterflies in your stomach make your head spin too! By participating in mock interview sessions, accepting the friendly critique of your networking peers, and continuing to practice, practice, practice, you will reduce those butterflies considerably and be able to walk into any job interview with confidence.

6

Sharpening Your Personal Appeal

Your interviews are drawing near, and you're probably feeling pretty confident after all those mock interview sessions and role-playing rehearsals. That's good, because what you say during the interview is crucial. There's something else to consider, however, and that is what you *don't say*. This is known as the *Silent Language* or *Subtext*. Subtext is a powerful force that can contradict what you say; likewise, it can reinforce your statements.

Monitor Your Subtext

Your subtext is revealed through your posture, eye contact, subtle gestures, the sound of your voice, the rhythm of your speech, your handshake, your dress, your facial expressions, and your personal grooming. This silent language is so dynamic that it can actually alter the hiring panel's perception of you.

To give you a graphic illustration, observe any court trial and you will notice that the defense attorney has altered the defendant's subtext to sway the jury. If a man has been accused of rape, for example, you can be sure he will appear in court wearing a beautifully tailored, conservative business suit, a pressed white shirt, and a "sincere" tie. His hair will be cut and styled, his fingernails will be clean and trimmed, and his earring will be stuffed into one of his pockets. He will also *appear* to be relaxed and confident, from his posture to his eye contact. The result of all this manipulation, his attorney hopes, is that at least one person on the jury will say, "He sure doesn't *look* like a rapist!"

In fact, many studies have concluded that any attractive, well-dressed defendant is favored by the jury because they are *perceived* as less likely to be guilty.

Or there is the example of a girl who attended a large city high school. She ran with a gang of girls she called "punks," who all spiked their hair, wore blue lipstick, and pierced their tongues. None of them was doing well in school. The girl wondered if her grades would improve if she changed her image, so she took some drastic measures. Not only did she do away with the hair spikes, blue lipstick, and tongue jewelry, but she toned down her wardrobe. Bingo! Her grades began to improve. Her efforts changed her image not only in the eyes of her teachers, but in her own eyes as well. Smart girl!

> *You only have one chance to make a first impression.*

Our purpose in this chapter is to make you aware of the subtle messages conveyed by your silent language, especially as they relate to your job interviews. You want members of hiring panels to like you at "first glance," from the moment you enter the room. Studies have shown, in fact, that your first impression will be a lasting impression: How you are perceived during that first 10 seconds is what people remember!

Dress and Grooming

Men should dress conservatively, in a business suit or a coordinated sport jacket and slacks. You should always wear a tie, but nothing faddish or novel.

> *"Dress as if you were seeking a promotion or a raise."*
>
> —Instructional coordinator and member of interview panel for a suburban school district in Virginia.

Women should wear a conservative suit or a dress, preferably with a classic line. A coat dress or one with a jacket is a good choice. Avoid anything that's too frilly, trendy, or "cute." Don't wear a pantsuit, because it may give the impression you're not taking the interview seriously. (You'll have plenty of chances to wear them once you're hired.) Also, avoid miniskirts and blouses that are frilly, off-the-shoulder, or low-cut.

Colors

Avoid bright colors or extremes. For men, dark blue and charcoal gray project a subtext of strength and competence. Black is considered too formal for a teaching interview; and tan should be avoided because it doesn't project confidence. Light gray is a possibility, depending on your coloring. A classic navy blazer with dark gray slacks is always a safe choice.

Men's shirts should be white, light gray, or blue. The tie should be tastefully muted in stripes, pin-dots, or a paisley. Be aware of your own coloring and choose a tie that gives you a feeling of self-confidence.

If you wear suspenders or braces, they should match the color of your tie (although they should be completely covered by your jacket).

The most important thing is that you select something that makes you feel good about yourself. If you feel good about yourself and you like the way you look, this image will be projected to the hiring panel.

Women may choose from a range of conservative colors. If you're undecided, you can't go wrong with navy blue. Feeling good about yourself is the most important factor, so try on several outfits before the interview, then choose the one that creates the strongest self-image.

Shoes

Be sure your shoes are shined and in good repair. Don't wear shoes with rundown heels or a worn, "cracked" look. Be sure your shoes go with your dress or suit. And don't let your shoes "dress you down." By that we mean that the style of your shoes should be as dressy as the clothes you are wearing. A pair of sandals, for example, would destroy the classic look of a conservative business suit.

Jewelry

Go easy on the jewelry. For men, a wedding ring and a wristwatch are plenty. If you wear an earring or a stud in your ear (or anywhere else that's visible), remove it for the interview.

Women should wear conservative gold, silver, or pearl earrings; avoid anything dangling or faddish. One ring on each hand is fine, plus a bracelet and a watch. If you wear an earring or a stud in your nose, lip, cheek, or tongue, remove it for the interview.

Cleanliness

Your body should be squeaky clean and odor-free, and your clothes should be clean, as well. Don't wear anything to the interview that has a spot or a stain (including sweat stains).

Before the interview, examine your clothes carefully in a strong light; if you have the slightest doubt about whether a spot will show, have the garment laundered or dry cleaned. Also look for any tears or moth holes that should be mended.

This is all just common sense, of course, but it's amazing how many stories we've heard of candidates who wore crumpled, soiled clothing to interviews. One interviewer told us about a woman who came to the interview wearing a dress that had both arm pits torn out—not a great first impression!

Men's fingernails should be trimmed and clean. Women should trim their nails to a conservative length, at least for the interview, and wear a neutral color of nail polish. Avoid bright reds, bright pinks, greens, blues, blacks, and nail art.

Hair

Men should have their hair cut or trimmed before the interview, including beards or mustaches. Facial hair is fine, but keep it groomed.

Women should wear their hair in a conservative style, and make sure it is clean and shiny. If you have very long hair, it might be a good idea to tie it back or pull it up onto your head for the interview. Most image experts advise against wearing long hair down over a business suit.

Makeup

Women should use makeup conservatively for the interview. Avoid too much eyeliner, mascara, and blusher, and wear lipstick in a pink, coral, or red—something that coordinates with your outfit. Stay away from blues, greens, blacks, and purples.

Body Language

In the course of our surveys, we had a very interesting interview with a behavioral specialist who sits on interview committees for a suburban school district in New Hampshire. When asked what she learned from a teacher-candidate's body language during interviews, she answered this way:

"I look for body language that demonstrates self-confidence. I want strong eye contact, a firm hand shake, and open posture. I look for movement that indicates uneasiness when new information is presented. I like it when I am able to read the

applicant's reaction to information I present. Often, when job duties or responsibilities are presented, the candidate's mouth is saying 'yes,' but the body language clearly indicates that he or she is not receptive to the job. This helps in screening out some candidates.

"*The more nervous and 'fidgety' applicant will almost never get the job. Those who appear at ease, comfortable, and relaxed will always come out on top.*"

—Director of bands and music curriculum and member of interview committee for a rural school district in Texas

"*I also like to see how the body responds under pressure. The body language at the interview will give me insight as to what I can expect in the future. In addition, a friendly smile is always welcome. After all, they will be working with children and we don't want them to be frightened.*"

This woman's insight is enormously valuable because it applies her expertise as a behavioral specialist to the field of education.

Eye Contact

We communicate with one another in many ways, but none is more important than eye contact. Eyes hold a world of emotions that are easily read.

When you're responding to a question during an interview, maintain eye contact with the members of the panel. Don't focus in on only one of the interviewers, but look from one to another. Direct eye contact implies honesty and sincerity. On the other hand, if your eyes are darting around the room as you speak, you take on a "shifty-eyed" look, which implies dishonesty. And whatever you do, don't stare at the ceiling, because that will send the message that you're bored.

Maintain direct eye contact with each panel member who is speaking, as well. This shows that you're interested and attentive to what the person is saying.

If you're one of those people who finds it difficult to look someone *straight* in the eye, talk to the person's eyebrows—no one will ever know the difference.

Facial Expressions

Did you know that your facial expressions can cause physiological reactions in your body? This was proven in a study by a team of psychologists at Clark University in Worcester, Massachusetts. If your face is screwed up tight with a look of anxiety, you will feel anxious. Likewise, if you concentrate on relaxing the muscles in your face, your body will react by relaxing all over. It's a cause-and-effect thing, with one feeding off the other.

Other facial expressions to avoid are frowns, "tight" lips, and squinted eyes; these all convey distrust or dislike for what is being said.

> *"Making eye contact is important. Also, how a person stands or walks can give hints to possible strengths or weaknesses."*
> —Instructional coordinator and member of interview committee for a suburban school district in Virginia

The bottom line is that you should work on keeping your facial expressions pleasant and relaxed, always ready for a smile when appropriate. A smile is a wonderful thing. An honest, sincere smile can convey enthusiasm, confidence, and control, even if you feel anything but enthusiastic, confident, or in control of the situation. It also will go a long way toward masking your nervousness and insecurities, and will put the interviewer at ease. A smile says, "I like you," "I agree with you," and "I'm happy and comfortable to be here."

The Handshake

As we mentioned earlier, there are three kinds of handshakes: limp, firm, and vice-grip. Obviously, a firm handshake is what you want to work on.

A limp handshake evokes many subtexts, none of them good: disinterest, insecurity, weakness, and nervousness. And the old-fashioned Victorian handshake that extends only the fingers is the most distasteful of all because it says, "I don't really want to touch you because I don't trust you."

A bone-crushing handshake, on the other hand, evokes a subtext of aggression and wanting to take control.

A proper handshake is one in which you extend your entire hand, grasp the hand of the other person "skin-to-skin," give it one firm shake, and then let go. Be sure to return the same amount of pressure as you're given; and don't hang on too long, or you'll give the impression that you're "taking over."

> *"I can feel the twinkle of his eye in his handshake."*
>
> —Helen Keller, after being introduced to Mark Twain

If shaking hands is awkward for you, now is the time to develop a firm, impressive grip. To do this, you will need to practice. Your small networking group is a good place to start, because all of you are in the same predicament, and you can all use the practice. If you make it a habit to shake hands with one another every time you get together, you will eventually feel comfortable with it. At that point you will be ready to graduate to the next step, which is to look the person in the eye and call him or her by name as you shake hands.

Keep practicing until it becomes second nature.

Posture

As you walk into the interview room, stand straight with your head held high; this shows that you're confident and happy to be there. On the other hand, if you enter the room slowly, with a shuffle and a lowered head, you give just the opposite impression.

The ideal posture during an interview is to sit up, lean forward with arms open, make eye contact, and smile, if appropriate. This is known as an "affirmative posture." A "negative posture" is one in which the interviewee slouches

> *"I usually look for someone who seems relaxed in the shoulders. Constant shifting or crossing and uncrossing legs can be distracting. I wouldn't hold it against someone, but if my choice was between someone who fidgeted a lot and someone who at least appeared collected, it would be no contest."*
>
> —8th-grade teacher and member of hiring committee for suburban district in Illinois

down in the chair, head down, arms crossed tightly at the waist, making no eye contact.

If an interviewer leans back as you're speaking, do the same. This indicates you may be coming on just a little strong. But be ready to lean forward again if you suddenly feel excited or passionate about something that's being said, or as soon as the interviewer leans forward and resumes an affirmative posture.

Hand Gestures

Hand gestures have a subtext all their own. Here are some common gestures you should avoid during a job interview:

- ✓ Stroking your chin
- ✓ Twisting your ear
- ✓ Scratching yourself—anywhere!
- ✓ Biting your nails
- ✓ Cracking your knuckles
- ✓ Pushing back your cuticles as you speak
- ✓ Jingling anything (keys, coins, etc.)
- ✓ Unwinding paper clips
- ✓ Fidgeting with or tapping a pen or pencil
- ✓ Playing with your rings, bracelet, earrings, or necklace
- ✓ Picking anything up and laying it back down

✓ Grooming yourself in any way (e.g., smoothing your clothing or picking lint off your sleeve)
✓ Smoothing your hair back
✓ Rubbing your eye
✓ Tugging at your collar
✓ Straightening or smoothing the knot in your tie
✓ Placing one hand on the back of your neck
✓ Crossing and uncrossing your fingers
✓ Fingering your throat
✓ Leaning back and placing both hands behind your head
✓ Clasping and unclasping your fingers
✓ Holding your fingers in front of your mouth
✓ Wringing your hands

These gestures are distracting and annoying, and they send dozens of different negative messages: nervousness, doubt, distaste, or the indication that you may be lying. One way to control your hands, of course, is to keep them tightly clasped together throughout the interview, but that isn't the best idea either, although it is a solution in extreme cases. The best thing is to let your hands fall naturally on the arms of the chair, or on the table if you're leaning forward, or (best of all) hold a pen in one hand, poised over your note pad.

> *"What I learn from an interviewee's body language is whether he or she really seems interested in the position or not."*
>
> —Science chair, mentor teacher, and member of interview committee for a rural school district in Northern California

Head Gestures

Head gestures are telling as well. A nod of the head sends a positive subtext: "Yes, I agree with what you're saying," or "I like you." A shake of the head, on the other hand, gives the impression that you don't like the person, or you don't like what is being said. Be careful that you don't nod your head constantly, however, or you will send a senseless subtext. Wait until you agree with something that is being said, then nod. The head nod is very effective if used with discretion.

Feet and Leg Gestures

Here are some feet and leg gestures to avoid during an interview:

- ✓ Shuffling your feet back and forth
- ✓ Shuffling your foot in and out of a shoe
- ✓ Tapping a foot
- ✓ Swinging a crossed leg back and forth
- ✓ Crossing and uncrossing your legs

If you're sitting at a table during the interview, feet and leg gestures aren't nearly as obvious as your hand and head gestures. Be aware of them, however, and try to keep your feet and legs still.

> *"We look for energy and enthusiasm. Are they smiling? Do they appear to have a sense of humor? Are they nervous? Do they wiggle in their seat?"*
> —A physics teacher and acting science department chair in Western New York

Voice and Speech

You will be doing a lot of talking during your interview, so it's important that you have a pleasant, well-modulated voice. When you are being interviewed for a job, there is a natural tendency for your pitch to get higher and higher; so make a concerted effort to lower your voice to a richly modulated tone. Then raise your voice off and on to make a point, always returning to the lower pitch. Whatever you do, don't speak in a monotone.

Speed of Speech

Nervousness not only causes your pitch to rise, it causes "fast talk," too. The more nervous you are, the faster you will talk. Rushing your words will reveal insecurity with your answers, embarrassment, awkwardness, or a message that you "just want to get this interview over with as soon as possible." Conversely, someone who speaks slowly conveys confidence, sincerity, and a feeling of being comfortable with the interview.

> "An interviewee's body language tells me how comfortable he is, what really excites him, if he is unsure of himself. A person who knows what's he's talking about and is excited about it leans forward, smiles more, and makes eye contact."
>
> —A member of an interview committee for an inner-city school district in Detroit

Patterns of Speech

Everyone has a certain cadence or pattern to their speech, punctuated with pauses, which are often effective, or with annoying fillers, which are not. Common fillers include phrases like, "You know," "Uhhh," "I mean," and clearing of the throat. Chances are you use fillers when you speak and don't even realize it. The only way you'll know for sure is to listen to yourself on an audio or videotape; you'll probably be surprised at all the fillers. Try to eliminate them as much as possible before you start interviewing. Ask your family, friends, and the members of your networking group to point them out if they sneak in unawares.

Use the information in this chapter to sharpen your personal appeal. Of course, you won't know what needs sharpening until you see yourself as others see you, and this is where your networking group comes in. Use the videotaped mock interviews to scrutinize one another's dress, grooming, body language, and voice patterns. Once you're aware of your flaws, it won't be difficult to correct them.

7

Your Conduct During the Interview

We could compare the job search to running a 1500 meter race . . . four laps around the track. By the end of the first lap you've located the job openings; by the end of lap two you've completed the paperwork; and if you survive the third lap of the race, you've made the paper cut and you're ready for that final gut-wrenching lap: the interview itself.

If you're one of eight contestants in the race, your chances of winning the gold medal depend on one final thing—how you conduct yourself during the interview.

A Positive Attitude Is the Key

Walk through any bookstore, and you will see hundreds of books on the impact of a positive attitude, including the ever-popular *The Power of Positive Thinking,* by Norman Vincent

Peale. Countless motivational speakers have touted its virtues for decades. There's a reason for this: Your attitude is the key to your success.

Jack Nicklaus in his book, *Golf My Way*,[1] even tells us that positive imaging can improve your golf game. For example, if you picture your ball lying 250 yards off the tee, right in the center of the fairway, it is much more likely to happen than if you scold yourself with negative talk, such as, "Don't lift your head" or "Don't top the ball." This kind of talk, in fact, produces exactly the result you didn't want, because it is the last thought you have before hitting the golf ball.

> *"Tell yourself that you are the best applicant and then go with confidence to the interview feeling prepared to be their next new hire!"*
> —Science chair, mentor teacher, and member of interview committee for a rural district in Northern California

So, the key is to have a positive attitude, always expecting the best to happen. But how can this help you during your job interview? Well, what works in golf also works in life. If you picture yourself doing well and being chosen to fill the position, it is more likely to happen.

Most candidates enter the interview room feeling like they are going on trial—as if the interview panel will sit in judgment of how they perform. If there is a table between the candidate and the panel—which there usually is—it creates an even greater barrier. However, the truth of the matter is this:

✓ **You are *not* on trial!**
  - The table that sits between you is only a *perceived* barrier
  - The panel wants to *help* you
  - They *want* you to sell yourself
  - They *want* you to be the one they hire

You see, they're on your side; it's not an adversarial situation. They want to find a terrific teacher to fill the vacancy, and they *hope* you're the one.

As you sit in the lobby waiting for your turn to be interviewed, remember that you must make a great first impression—there are no second chances. Think of how you feel sitting in an audience when an entertainer or comedian steps on stage; it only takes 10 seconds to know whether you like the person or not.

> *"Speak from your heart . . . your love for children will come through."*
> —High school special education teacher in Wisconsin

It's the same way with a job interview. You have to make them like you in the first 10 seconds—no retakes, no second chances. So visualize yourself doing just that, and then, as your name is called and you walk into the interview room, stand straight, hold your head high, shake hands, and smile as you look each panel member straight in the eye.

Questions You Should Ask

At some point during the interview, you will be expected to ask questions of your own. Often, interviewees take a somewhat defensive role, merely listening and responding to the questions asked by the panel. Depending on how comfortable you are, you may not feel like breaking in with a question of your own. Then again, depending on how things are going, you may feel at ease to ask a question at any point.

In either case, you definitely want to have questions prepared beforehand. If your questions are not answered in the course of the interview, be sure to ask them before you conclude. Typically, toward the end of the interview, the panel will ask if you have any questions. At this point an answer such as, "No, I think you've answered them all" or "No, I can't think of anything" is not going to look good. They

> *"Don't be afraid to ask questions. Prepare some, even on a card, so that you appear to be well-prepared."*
>
> —*8th-grade teacher and member of hiring committee for suburban district in Illinois*

expect you to be curious about things, and if you've thought this out in advance, it will impress them.

Don't rely on memory for these important questions. Practice asking them out loud before the day of the interview, then jot them down on a 3" x 5" card and bring the card with you to the interview. The interview panel will be impressed that you put some forethought into the interview process.

Before getting into examples of questions you might want to ask, we want to caution you on being *too* aggressive with your questioning. Keep in mind that you are the interviewee. Yes it's true, you are interviewing them, too. You want to find out if the job is a good fit. And using your mission statement as a guide, there are certain things you

> *"Jot down any questions that come to mind during the interview itself."*
>
> —*8th-grade teacher and member of hiring committee for suburban district in Illinois*

must learn about the position, the school, the district, and so on. But remember to ask your questions in such a way that you don't give the impression you are "taking over" the interview.

Also, there are certain kinds of questions we recommend avoiding; these we'll talk about a little later in this chapter.

Ask Questions That Showcase Your Talents

Back to the questions you will want to ask: There's a little twist that can work for you just as well as it works for the interview panel. We mentioned in chapter 5 that interviewers' questions often have underlying purposes. For example, when they ask, "What are your strengths and weaknesses?" or "Tell us about yourself," what they really want to know is, "Why should we hire you?" Well, there's no reason your questions can't have an underlying purpose as well: that is, to showcase your talents. Here are a few examples of questions you might ask:

✓ I've had some experience working on a school yearbook, and I really enjoyed working with the students. Do you have a yearbook?

✓ I've always considered myself a team player and feel it's important and more productive when staff members can put their heads together. Do the teachers at this school plan or work on projects together?

✓ I have experience in choral music and play production and would like to be involved in that in some way. Does your school offer any music or drama for the kids or the community?

The underlying purpose of these questions is to show that you have talents that can be of benefit to the school and the community. They also demonstrate that you are an enthusiastic team player, willing to give more time and energy than any of the other candidates being interviewed by the panel.

There are other questions you can ask that might impress the panel. These questions demonstrate your knowledge, enthusiasm, and interest. When we asked interview panel members what questions they felt teacher-candidates should ask during an interview, we got these suggestions:

1. **In what ways do the parents get involved with the school?**

2. **What kinds of cross-cultural activities do you offer to the kids and the community (assuming an ethnic diversity exists)?**

3. **What new innovations or programs has the school or the district implemented (for your grade level or subject area)?**

4. Does the school or district have a general discipline plan (e.g., Canter & Canter, *Assertive Discipline*)?

5. Does the school or district have a mentor teacher program?

6. Are the classrooms self-contained or departmentalized?

7. Is there team teaching?

8. Do you offer professional growth opportunities for new teachers?

9. What are the strengths of this school/district?

10. How do administrators offer teacher support if the need arises?

11. How would you characterize school morale?

12. When will you be notifying candidates of your hiring decisions?

> *"Don't ever ask a direct question of a certain individual sitting on the hiring panel. It puts the person on the spot."*
>
> —California school administrator and member of hiring panel

This is not an exhaustive list; it is meant to suggest some ideas for you to consider. Some may not seem important or applicable to you, but because they were suggested by members of hiring panels, we think they should be given some weight.

One great piece of advice came from a school principal we interviewed, who said that the teacher-candidate should *never* address a specific member of the panel. For example, you should never ask, "Ms. Johnson, what is your district's policy regarding bilingual education?"

This is a mistake for several reasons. First, Ms. Johnson may not know about the policy, or there may not be a specific policy. Also, Ms. Johnson may not agree with the district's philosophy of bilingual education, which could result in a very awkward moment for everyone. The results of this kind of questioning leave Ms. Johnson looking bad and feeling embarrassed, which means the candidate scores badly.

If you think a question is legitimate, you should ask it, of course; but direct it to the entire committee. One word of advice: Always ask sincere questions that are *important to you*. If your questions impress the interview committee or give you a chance to tell them something more about yourself, that is simply an added bonus.

The important thing to remember is this: You should come prepared with a few well-thought-out questions; that will impress the interview panel.

Questions to Avoid

Just as important as the questions you ask are those you don't. There are some questions you should simply avoid asking. Most of these are fairly obvious. But, according to our hiring panel contacts throughout the United States, a few words should be mentioned here about indiscreet, inappropriate questions. Then there are those questions that are not necessarily indiscreet or inappropriate, but that, in a subtle way, can put you on thin ice and work against you.

Before we list the questions to avoid, however, let us mention one caveat that applies to your whole demeanor, including your questions of the hiring panel: That is the matter of *attitude*. If your attitude is perceived as even slightly questionable, it probably will undo all the positives you've worked so hard to develop and communicate. We don't want you to mess up a good thing because of a slip of the tongue or an indiscretion. So avoid any question that makes your attitude suspect. If there is something you think you really must ask and you're unsure how it will be taken, use your own judgment; but conventional wisdom would say—forget it. Or reword it so that the attitude factor is taken out of the mix. You get the point.

Sometimes it's not so much the question itself, but something in the inflection or tone of your voice or in your body language that may tip your hand in the minds of the panel and work against you. You only get one shot at this stuff, so choose your words *and your tone* carefully.

With that sermonette preached, let's move on to a list of questions or topics we think should be avoided. Most of them have come from principals, mentor teachers, curriculum personnel, and others who sit on hiring panels in their districts.

The most obvious topics to avoid are at the top of the list:

1. **Anything related to salary**
2. **Benefits** (School office personnel, your teacher association representative, or a teacher handbook can fill you in on this subject.)
3. **School hours** (This information can be obtained from the school secretary or by asking other teachers. Most schools have a standard school day: start at 8:30 or 9 A.M.; dismiss at 3 or 3:30 P.M.)
4. **Time off for personal family consideration** (Don't ask the members of the panel, get a copy of the school's teacher handbook.)
5. **Breakdown of ethnicity of the community** (Unless, of course, you're a bilingual teacher and this information is necessary.)
6. **Anything remotely sexist**
7. **Any question that could be interpreted to mean that you're not totally committed to the teaching profession** (For example, "Do you expect your teachers to take work home often?")
8. **Over-stressing concerns regarding discipline** (Don't ask question after question about discipline-related issues.)
9. **Any questions that pertain to the religious, political, or socioeconomic breakdown of the community** (You get into touchy areas here, and the chances are too great that your questions will be misread. This information is available through other sources.)

10. **Questions regarding the "bargaining unit"** (You're talking to the wrong folks if you bring up unions or teachers' associations here.)

11. **Extracurricular responsibilities** (Don't ask anything that may cause the panel to question your work ethic or attitude.)

12. **Prospects of transferring to another grade level or department** (Wait until you're hired; then pursue this concern at the appropriate time.)

37 Ways to Turn Off an Interview Committee

We asked every interviewer who took part in our survey 20 or so questions, including this one: "What is the biggest turn-off during an interview?" Some of the answers were what we expected to hear, but others were quite surprising.

1. **Inappropriate clothing/dress**

   Women will never go wrong wearing a nice dress or suit; men should wear slacks and a sport jacket or a business suit, depending on the school district, always with a tie. We were shocked at the number of times "unshined shoes" cropped up. Don't just dust them off—*shine them!*

2. **Giving pat, canned, or insincere answers**

   Interview committees can read these like a book. We suggest you practice pausing at least a second or two before responding to any question. This gives the impression that you are thoughtful, relaxed, and poised. Practice responding to the sample questions listed in chapter 5 until your answers sound as natural and unrehearsed as possible. Finally, be honest.

3. **Poor communication of ideas**

   One cause for this is a lack of practice at responding to possible panel questions. Even if you have thought out a response in advance, you might still be unable to articulate it clearly. Again, we suggest practice, practice, practice.

4. **Blaming students for their failure to do well**

   It's hard to imagine that teachers would blame students for their lack of success when one of their jobs is to motivate students. The school and teacher can and do make a difference. Don't be an "elitist-defeatist."

5. **Not knowing when to close or to stop talking**

   Often, the more you ramble on, the more you paint yourself into a corner. By rambling on and on you reveal either (1) that you don't really know the answer, but with enough tries you hope to stumble upon it, or (2) that you are unable to express yourself succinctly. Hiring committees are seldom interested in soliloquies. They appreciate a brief, concise, well-articulated response.

> *"Strange how much you've got to know, before you know how little you know."*
> —Author unknown

6. **Chewing gum or smoking during the interview**

   While this is hard to believe, interviewers tell us it does happen. Gum chewing may be an oversight; ditch your gum before you leave home. Two thoughts about smoking: (1) If you can't make it through an interview without a smoke, how are you going to teach for hours at a time? (2) If teachers are role models, what example are you setting for students when you smoke?

7. **An attitude that is too relaxed and informal**

   It's good to be relaxed, but familiarity can be over-done and work against you. You don't want to appear disinterested in the questions or disrespect-ful to the panel members.

8. **Answers that are too defensive or aggressive**

   Either of these creates an awkward, uncomfortable interview. Interviews are not meant to be confronta-tional. Don't come to the interview with an "atti-tude."

9. **Dangling earrings or long, brightly painted fingernails**

   We found that many interviewers aren't crazy about either one of these. In one case, a teacher with long, painted nails was being interviewed for a kindergar-ten position. None of the panel members could picture her working with 5- or 6-year-olds, so they hired someone else. As far as earrings go, you might opt for a pair of conservative gold or silver studs instead.

10. **Trying to unduly impress the interview com-mittee with boundless knowledge giving the impression that you're an expert on all educa-tional topics**

    Don't go by the old expression, "If you've got it, flaunt it!" Your responses will reveal your command of the subject matter. "Selling yourself" has its limits—don't carry on *ad nauseam*. The committee can tell the difference between a phony and the real thing. A little knowledge can be dangerous, so play it safe.

11. **Indications that you think your methods and philosophies are the only ones**

This is closely related to number 10, and the same advice applies: Watch it, or you'll appear arrogant. Don't insult the panel: They've been around much longer than you have. You must have opinions and some understanding of teaching methods, but remember, you're just getting started in this profession.

12. **Lack of membership in professional organizations**

Memberships in professional organizations are very impressive. They show you have interest, enthusiasm, and professionalism. Most professional organizations are there to help you; get acquainted with them. (We've included a list of such organizations in the appendix.) Be prepared to drop a few names, if possible. This is definitely an opportunity to give yourself a leg up; take advantage of it.

13. **Candidates who think they have finished learning because they are out of school**

This kind of attitude displays inflexibility. Learning should be a lifelong mission for everyone—especially those in the teaching profession. It also calls your work ethic into question.

14. **Bragging, going beyond reasonable selling of yourself; flaunting yourself**

Again, if you're good, you don't have to prove it through arrogance or a haughty manner. Rest assured, the interview committee knows the difference between confidence and an overbearing, obnoxious "sales job."

15. **Criticizing or badmouthing another school, district, or person, including a previous employer**

This has never helped anyone get a job—in *any* profession. Everything you say may be true, but it doesn't help your cause. The committee will simply assume you'll badmouth their school if they hire you.

16. **Not knowing current educational trends, methods, and issues**

Being new to the profession, you won't be expected to know *all* the new and current things going on, but you should definitely know the "hottest" ones. Be prepared to name-drop on occasion. A "clueless look" in response to a question will be a red flag to the committee.

17. **No knowledge of the school or community**

Do your homework: Know something about the basic demographics of the school and the community (see chapter 5).

18. **Displaying stupidity in questions asked and responses given**

Never ask questions about salary and benefits. And avoid asking questions that reveal you know nothing at all about the school district or the community. If you're asked a question and you know absolutely nothing about the subject, don't wing it; it is better to say you don't know the answer than to insult the committee by blowing smoke.

19. **Poor grammar**

Is your grammar adequate? If your best friend won't tell you, then ask someone else—someone who will be completely honest. If colloquial family or regional grammar problems crop up in your speech, you need to be aware of and correct them. Poor grammar can be a *real* handicap.

20. Poor personal hygiene

If that smell wasn't there before you arrived, and if it disappears when you leave, you're in big trouble. Poor personal hygiene is inexcusable. Most people are offended by it. We can't imagine a candidate coming to an interview with bad breath or body odor, yet it happens. Don't be one of these losers. You'll never get that job—count on it.

21. Lackluster performance

If a member of the committee checks your vital signs at any time during the interview, assume you're not doing well. Be upbeat and positive. A little nervousness is normal, but put that adrenaline to good use. Schools need intelligent, dynamic teachers. Present that image.

22. Negative body language

As we discussed in chapter 6, negative body language can include everything from a closed position to poor eye contact, slouching, a defensive posture, or a scowl. Sit in a relaxed, comfortable fashion. Make eye contact with the person asking the question; then make eye contact with the rest of the members of the panel as you answer the question. Be pleasant and sincere.

23. Being unprepared

In addition to being prepared to answer the panel's questions, bring your portfolio to the interview, along with 3" x 5" cards that have questions to ask at the end of the interview. Also bring a pen and note paper, preferably affixed inside a manila folder. And plan to arrive at least 10 minutes early for your interview.

24. Those who have no questions for the interview panel

If you're *really* interested in working at a particular school, you should have some specific, intelligent questions to ask about that school. Your questions will show the panel that you're interested in knowing more and will give them a chance to brag a little—definitely good PR.

25. Negativity by the candidate

Interview panels *do not* enjoy interviewing negative candidates, and negative candidates almost *never* get the jobs. Schools are looking for positive, upbeat teachers. Avoid negativity.

26. Body piercing

If you normally wear a ring or a stud in your tongue, lip, nose, or eyebrow, you might want to remove it before an interview. Although this is a fashionable trend and you're certainly entitled to pierce your body if you want to, you should be aware that, at least in our survey, body piercing is often a major turn-off to interviewers.

27. Inflexibility

Because teachers work in an environment with so many variables, they must be flexible. Schedules change, interruptions happen, equipment fails, employees don't show, children get sick—the list is endless. If you appear to be a team player who isn't easily flustered, you will have a much better chance of being hired.

28. Lack of self-confidence

It's natural to feel apprehensive and a little short on confidence in a stressful, unfamiliar setting; and interviews certainly fall into that category. To overcome this, we suggest you come to the interview as prepared as possible. Spend time in advance rehearsing your responses to questions you might be asked, and practice role-playing a few mock interviews (see chapter 5). These exercises will help you feel more confident during the interview.

If your self-confidence is still a little shaky when you arrive for the interview, you can usually give the *impression* of confidence by replacing your anxious frown with a sincere smile.

29. Tardiness

To land a job, you need every advantage—and the last time we checked, tardiness wasn't one of them. First impressions are lasting impressions; being late makes a bad first impression.

We suggest you arrive early enough to visit the restroom and check your appearance. (You never know, you may have a piece of spinach hanging from a tooth, smudged eye shadow, or something unbuttoned.) Remember, tardiness is a form of rudeness. Don't be rude.

30. Being political or contacting a member of the interview committee away from the interview setting

Members of an interview committee act collectively. Even if you know a member of the committee—or you know someone who knows someone who knows someone on the committee—you must not skirt the process by trying to influence an individual panel member. This puts that person in an awkward position and may well backfire on you. Go through the process like everyone else, and avoid the temptation to make political contacts to better your cause.

31. Haughty, arrogant, or superior manner

To mask insecurity some people *act* haughty, arrogant, or superior; others *are* haughty, arrogant, and think they're superior. Whichever the case, such behavior will count as a strike against you. You need to be a bit humble in this situation, even though you are trying to sell yourself. Remember: You don't have a job—they do.

32. Showing more interest in the compensation package than in the kids

Unless the interview committee brings it up, *never* ask about salary or fringe benefits. These are public knowledge and readily available by other means.

33. Those who make a point of what they won't do (or the "not my job" syndrome)

You are interviewing for a position that has certain expectations. If you make it a point to tell the committee which duties you would rather not perform, they will be relieved to hear about them—so they can hire someone else. Hiring panels are looking for workers, not shirkers.

34. Telling the committee what you think they want to hear

If you're so desperate for a job that your answers reflect only what you think they want to hear, rather than what you really feel, you may end up with a job you're unhappy with; and the district ends up with an employee they wished they hadn't hired.

35. Not sticking to the subject, birdwalking

When answering questions, be concise; resist the temptation to impress the panel with your wealth of college knowledge. Stick to the subject and don't say anything that doesn't improve upon the silence.

36. Lack of passion for kids and teaching

Teaching is not just a job—it's a way of life. When you talk to the interview committee, they should see someone who is excited about the profession. Your body language should show it; your words should tell it; your eyes should flash it. Good teachers are usually good performers, too. Show some passion!

37. Poor social skills

Review the "don'ts" from the last chapter, including poor eye contact, "dressing down," and covering your mouth as you speak. Work on a firm, steady handshake.

In this chapter we have given you lots of "Do's" and "Don'ts." Be aware of the latter, but don't dwell on them. Emphasize instead the "Do's" and remember: you're a strong candidate or you wouldn't have made it this far.

If you run this final lap in style—if your attitude is great, your questions appropriate, and your responses impressive and tactful, you're sure to win the race.

Finally, at the conclusion of your interview, stand, smile, thank the panel for the opportunity to interview, and walk confidently from the room with visions of the gold medal that will surely be yours once the race results are posted.

Notes

1. *Golf My Way* by Jack Nicklaus (New York: Simon and Schuster, 1974).

8

After the Interview

The job search process doesn't end with the interview. You can still influence the hiring panel in two important ways—by sending a thank-you letter and placing a follow-up phone call.

The Thank-You Letter

Be sure to follow up the interview with a thank-you letter. Not only is this proper etiquette, it's a very smart thing to do. It is a way of gently reminding the interviewer who you are. If a dozen or so applicants were interviewed for the position, you should take this opportunity to sell yourself one more time. You may be the only applicant who makes this effort, and it will create a positive impression, especially if you're already near the top of the list.

Write the letter as soon as possible, preferably the same day you are interviewed. You want your letter to arrive *before* the decision is made. After all, proper etiquette isn't the *only* reason you're sending it; you hope it will sway the panel.

This is the structure of a good thank-you letter:

✓ **Paragraph 1:** Thank the interviewer for considering you for the position. Mention something specific you especially appreciated about the meeting.

✓ **Paragraph 2:** Tactfully review your qualifications and how you feel they are a match for the position.

✓ **Paragraph 3:** Thank the interviewer for his or her time and express your continued interest in the position.

Here is an example of a well-written thank-you letter:

Carson MacAllister
8506 Turner Avenue
Indianapolis, IN 46226

February 27, 1997

Dr. Martin Stuart
Superintendent
Hammond Unified School District
932 Palerma Avenue
Hammond, IN 47301

Dear Dr. Stuart:

Thank you for meeting with me today to discuss the position you have available for a seventh-grade language arts teacher.

It was encouraging to hear of your recent purchase of Macintosh computers and the new Edgar Writing Skills software. As we discussed during our conversation, I have had a great deal of experience using this software in the past, and it would be exciting for me to be involved in your new program. It will be rewarding to see how quickly your students' writing skills will improve.

Again, many thanks for your time and attention. I am very interested in your school district and would enjoy working at Montbello School as your new language arts teacher. I look forward to hearing from you in the near future.

Sincerely,

Carson MacAllister

Follow-Up Phone Calls

It's also a smart idea to follow up your interview and thank-you letter with a telephone call. In fact, certain situations demand it:

- ✓ If you have additional or recent information that may sway the decision in your favor.
- ✓ You wrote a thank-you letter, but haven't heard anything for two weeks.
- ✓ You have received another job offer and need to know where you stand before making the decision.
- ✓ You feel the interview went badly, and you want to request a second interview.

Before you place the call, brace yourself for the possibility that they have hired someone else without notifying you. If this happens, you should try to find out why they hired someone else. Ask what you can do to improve your interview skills in the future.

Some administrators will give you helpful advice—if you ask. But don't expect them to tell you why you weren't hired. Lawsuits have been initiated over such information, and administrators are told not to discuss personnel decisions. Now, if you're mentally prepared to make that call, here are some ideas of what you might say:

"Dr. Stuart? This is Carson MacAllister. We met on February 27th, when I was interviewed for the seventh-grade language arts position at Montbello School. I wanted to know if you've reached your decision. . . . "

If the decision has not been made, you might want to add something like this to your conversation:

"I've had some ideas on how we might expand the Edgar Writing Skills Program to help the eighth graders as well. I would like to meet with you again to talk about this possibility. . . . "

Or:

"Is there anything further you would like to know about me that might help you with your decision?"

Or:

"Do you know when you will make your decision? I have another job offer pending, but I would like to know if I am still being considered for the position at your school."

If you have no doubt that your interview went badly, you might be up front with the interviewer and ask if you can meet again:

"Dr. Stuart, I don't feel the interview afforded you the opportunity to see my full potential. Would it be possible for me to stop by to talk to you once more before you make your decision?"

Of the teacher-candidates and newly hired teachers in our survey, 37 percent said they followed up their interviews with a thank-you letter and/or a telephone call.

By the way, if the position is filled, don't give up. Keep calling back, reminding the interviewer who you are and that you're still interested in other positions that open up in the future. You might have been a very close second. You never know, vacancies occur at odd times throughout the year, and you might just be the one who gets the job because of your persistence.

Be Patient and Positive

If you haven't been offered a position even after several interviews that seemed to go well, try not to get discouraged. Research shows that people often receive many rejections before finally being hired. If you've had a number of rejections so far, keep looking ahead—the next interview may well result in a "Yes."

Don't let the rejections get you down; there are many reasons that someone else may have been hired that have nothing to do with you personally. There may have been three or four candidates who were equally qualified for the position, but one may have had something as simple as an additional credential that would give the school district more options in the future. And if you interviewed for a position as a high school history/geography teacher, maybe they hired the one candidate who had been on three European tours (as opposed to your one). That's not a reflection on you: That merely reflects your bad luck in competing against someone so well-traveled.

So don't beat yourself up and fill your mind with defeatist thoughts; if you do, those thoughts will grow and multiply, feeding on each other until your mind is so full of them that hope doesn't have a chance. If you are to keep your hopes alive, keep your mind clear of anything negative.

Don't let your dream of becoming a teacher die. You have a chance to be a life-changing influence in young lives. You've worked too hard for this, and it's too worthy a profession to abandon at this early stage. All it takes is a little patience, a little prayer, and a little time. It will come . . . and soon. We wish you much success!

> *"Don't lose hope. I was told by every interviewer that I was an exceptional candidate, then told that I was their second choice. If you really want to teach, if you can't picture yourself doing anything else, then you will eventually teach. I look back and am thankful I was able to resist the temptation to give up."*
> —High school social studies teacher in New Jersey

Epilogue

Now you know the "inside secrets" of finding a teaching position, and you're sure to be the one who stands out from the rest, landing not just one but several job offers! Our hearts go with you in your pursuit. You're going to love being a teacher: It's a rewarding, life-changing profession, the noblest of them all.

Perhaps Lee Iacocca said it best:

"In a completely rational society, the best of us would aspire to be teachers and the rest of us would have to settle for something less, because passing civilization along from one generation to the next ought to be the highest honor and the highest responsibility anyone could have."

Hang in there—it's worth it!

Jack Warner & Clyde Bryan

Bibliography

Albert, L. (1991) *A Teacher's Guide to Cooperative Discipline*. Circle Pines, MN: American Guidance Service.

Bolles, R. N. (1994) *What Color Is Your Parachute?* Berkeley, CA: Ten Speed Press

Canter, L., and Canter, M. (1992) *Assertive Discipline*. Santa Monica, CA: Canter and Associates.

Charles, C. M. (1989) *Building Classroom Discipline: From Models to Practice*. White Plains, NY: Longman.

Curwin, R. L., and A. N. Mendler (1989) *Discipline with Dignity*. Alexandria, VA: Association for Supervision and Curriculum Development.

Duffy, P., and T. Walter Wannie (1995) *Landing a Job*. Indianapolis: JIST Works.

Eggert, M. (1992) *The Perfect Interview*. Avenel, NJ: Wings Books.

Emmer, E. T., C. M. Evertson, J. P. Sanford, B. S. Clements, and M. E. Worsham (1984) *Classroom Management for Secondary Teachers*. New York: Prentice-Hall.

Englander, M. E. (1986) *Strategies for Classroom Discipline*. Westport, CT: Praeger.

Evans, W. H., S. S. Evans, and R. E. Schmid (1989) *Behavioral and Instructional Management*. New York: Allyn & Bacon.

Evertson, C. M., E. T. Emmer, B. S. Clements, J. P. Sanford, and M. E. Worsham (1984) *Classroom Management for Elementary Teachers*. New York: Prentice-Hall.

Farr, J. M., and S. Christophersen (1990) *An Introduction to Job Applications*. Indianapolis: JIST Works.

Farr, J. M. (1995) *Getting the Job You REALLY Want*. Indianapolis: JIST Works.

Farr, J. M. (1996) *The Quick Resume & Cover Letter Book*. Indianapolis: JIST Works.

Farr, J. M., and S. Christophersen (1990) *Why Should I Hire You?* Indianapolis: JIST Works.

Froyen, L. A. (1992) *Classroom Management: Empowering Teachers*. New York: Charles Merrill.

Jandt, F. E., and M. B. Nemnich (1997) *Using the Internet and the World Wide Web in Your Job Search*. Indianapolis: JIST Works.

Jones, F. H. (1987) *Positive Classroom Discipline*. New York: McGraw-Hill.

Keating, B., M. Pickering, B. Slack, and J. White (1989) *A Guide to Positive Discipline: Helping Students Make Responsible Choices*. New York: Allyn & Bacon.

Levin, J., and J. F. Nola (1995) *Principles of Classroom Management: A Hierarchal Approach*. New York: Prentice-Hall.

Nicklaus, J. (1974) *Golf My Way*. New York: Simon and Schuster.

Noble, D. F. (1995) *Gallery of Best Resumes*. Indianapolis: JIST Works.

Peale, N. V. (1992) *The Power of Positive Thinking*. Fawcett, NY: Crest Books.

Savage, T. V. (1990) *Discipline for Self-Control*. New York: Prentice-Hall.

Seeman, H. (1988) *Preventing Classroom Discipline Problems: A Guide for Educators*. Lancaster, PA: Technomic Publishing.

Sprick, R. S. (1985) *Discipline in the Secondary Classroom: A Problem-by-Problem Survival Guide*. Englewood Cliffs, NJ: Center for Applied Research in Education.

Steere, B. F. (1988) *Becoming an Effective Classroom Manager: A Resource for Teachers*. Albany: State University of New York Press.

Swanson, D. (1995) *The Resume Solution*. Indianapolis: JIST Works.

Walker, J. E., and T. M. Shay (1990) *Behavior Management: A Practical Approach for Educators*, 5th ed. New York: Macmillan.

Appendix
Education Resource Organizations

Educational Associations

American Alliance for Health, Physical
    Education, Recreation, and Dance
1900 Association Drive
Reston, VA 22091
(703) 476-3400

American Association for Gifted Children
Duke University
1121 W. Main St., Ste. 100
Durham, NC 27701
(919) 683-1400

American Association of Physics Teachers
5112 Berwyn Road
College Park, MD 20740
(301) 345-4200

American Counseling Assoc.
5999 Stevenson Ave.
Alexandria, VA 22304-3300
(703) 823-9800

American Federation of Teachers, AFL-CIO
555 New Jersey Ave., NW
Washington, DC 20001
(202) 879-4400

American Library Association
50 East Huron
Chicago, IL 60611
(312) 944-6780

American Mathematical Society
201 Charles Street
P.O. Box 6248
Providence, RI 02940
(401) 455-4000

American Montessori Society
150 Fifth Avenue
New York, NY 10011
(212) 924-3209

American Speech-Language-Hearing
    Association
10801 Rockville Pike
Rockville, MD 20852
(301) 897-5700

Association for Childhood Education
    International
11501 Georgia Ave., Suite 315
Wheaton, MD 20902
(301) 942-2443

Association for Teacher Educators
1900 Association Dr., Ste. ATE
Reston, VA 22091
(703) 620-3110

Council for Advancement & Support of
    Education
11 Dupont Circle, NW, Ste. 400
Washington, DC 20036
(202) 328-5900

Council for Children with Behavioral
    Disorders
c/o Council for Exceptional Children
1920 Association Drive
Reston, VA 22091-1589
(703) 620-3660

Council for Elementary Science
    International
212 Townsend Hall
Columbia, MO 65211
(314) 882-4831

Council for Exceptional Children
1920 Association Drive
Reston, VA 22091-1589
(703) 620-3660

Music Educators National Conference
1806 Robert Fulton Drive
Reston, VA 22091
(703) 860-4000

Music Teachers National Association
441 Vine Street, Ste. 505
Cincinnati, OH 45202-2814
(513) 421-1420

National Art Education Association
1916 Association Drive
Reston, VA 22091-1590
(703) 860-8000

National Association for Bilingual Education
Union Center Plaza
1220 L Street, NW, Ste. 605
Washington, DC 20005
(202) 898-1829

National Association for Business Teacher
    Education
1914 Association Drive
Reston, VA 22091
(703) 860-8300

National Association for the Education of
    Young Children
1509 16th Street, NW
Washington, DC 20036
(202) 232-8777

National Association of Biology Teachers
11250 Roger Bacon Drive, Ste. 19
Reston, VA 22090
(703) 471-1134

National Association of Industrial &
    Technical Teacher Educators
University of Tennessee
Technological & Adult Education
402 Claxton Addition
Knoxville, TN 37996-3400
(615) 974-2574

National Business Education Association
1914 Association Drive
Reston, VA 22091-1596
(703)860-8300

National Council for the Social Studies
3501 Newark Street, NW
Washington, DC 20016
(202) 966-7840

National Council of Teachers of English
111 Kenyon Road
Urbana, Illinois 61801-1096
(217) 328-3870

National Council of Teachers of
    Mathematics
1906 Association Drive
Reston, VA 22091-1593
(703) 620-9840

National Education Association
1201 16th Street, NW
Washington, DC 20036
(202) 833-4000

National Science Teachers Association
1742 Connecticut Avenue, NW
Washington, DC 20009-1171
(202) 328-5800

National Vocational Guidance Association
    (or National Career Development
    Association)
5999 Stevenson Avenue
Alexandria, VA 22304
(703) 823-9800

School Science and Mathematics Association
Curriculum and Foundations
Bloomsburg, PA 17815
(717) 389-4915

Speech Communication Association
5105 Blacklick Road, Bldg. E
Annandale, VA 22003
(703) 750-0533

Opportunities for Overseas Employment

Department of Defense Dependents School
Recruitment Unit
4040 N. Fairfax Drive
Arlington, VA 22203-1634

Fulbright Teacher Exchange Program
U.S. Information Agency
600 Maryland Avenue, SW, Rm. 235
Washington, DC 20024-2520
(800) 726-0479

Institute of International Education
Information and Reference Division
809 United Nations Plaza
New York, NY 10017

International School Service, Inc.
P.O. Box 5910
Princeton, NJ 08543
(609) 452-0990

Peace Corps of the United States
Box 941
Washington, DC 20526
(800) 424-8580, Ext. 2293

U.S. Department of State
Office of Overseas Schools
Rm. 234, SA-6
Washington, DC 20520

*For teaching opportunities in the following
   locations write to:*

American Samoa Department of Education
Pago-Pago, Tutulia
American Samoa 96799

Commonwealth of Puerto Rico
Department of Education
P.O. Box 759
Hato Rey, Puerto Rico 00919

Commonwealth of the Northern Mariana
   Islands
Board of Education
P.O. Box 1370 CK
Saipan, MP 96950

Guam Department of Education
P.O. Box DE
Agana, Guam 96910

Virgin Islands Department of Education
44-46 Kongens Gade
Charlotte Amalie, Virgin Islands 00802

*These associations and publications are
additional resources for educators seeking
jobs overseas:*

English Education Services International
   Newsletter
139 Massachusetts Avenue
Boston, MA 02115

The International Educator
P.O. Box 103
West Bridgewater, MA 02379
(508) 580-1880

Overseas Academic Opportunities
949 E. 29th Street, 2nd Floor
Brooklyn, NY 11210

Overseas Employment Information for
   Teachers
Department of State
Washington, DC 20520

Overseas Placement Service for Educators
University of Northern Iowa
Students Services Center #19
Cedar Falls, IA 50614
(319) 273-2061

Teachers Overseas Recruitment Center
National Teacher Placement Bureau
P.O. Box 609027
Cleveland, OH 44109
(216) 741-3771

TESOL Bulletin
Teaching English to Speakers of
   Other Languages
1600 Cameron Street, Suite 300
Alexandria, VA 22314

State Departments of Education

Alabama
Alabama Department of Education
Gordon Persons Office Building
50 North Ripley Street
Montgomery, AL 36130-3901
(334) 242-9977

Alaska
Alaska State Department of Education
Goldbelt Building
801 W. 10th Street, Ste. 200
Juneau, AK 99801-1894
(907) 465-2831

Arizona
Arizona Department of Education
1535 West Jefferson
Phoenix, AZ 85007
(602) 542-4368

Arkansas
Arkansas Department of Education
4 State Capitol Mall, Rm. 304-A
Little Rock, AR 72201-1071
(501) 682-4475

California
California Department of Education
721 Capitol Mall
P.O. Box 944272
Sacramento, CA 95814
(916) 445-7254

Colorado
Colorado Department of Education
201 East Colfax Avenue
Denver, CO 80203-1799
(303) 866-6628

Connecticut
Connecticut Department of Education
165 Capitol Avenue, Rm. 346
Hartford, CT 06145
(860) 566-4561

Delaware
Delaware Department of Public Instruction
Townsend Building
P.O. Box 1402
Dover, DE 19903
(302) 739-4688

District of Columbia
District of Columbia Public Schools
415 12th Street, NW
Washington, DC 20004
(202) 724-4250

Florida
Florida Department of Education
Capitol Building, Rm. PL 08
Tallahassee, FL 32301
(904) 488-1234

Georgia
Georgia Department of Education
2066 Twin Towers East
205 Butler Street
Atlanta, GA 30334-5020
(404) 656-2604

Hawaii
Hawaii Department of Education
1390 Miller Street #307
Honolulu, HI 96813
(808) 586-3420

Idaho
Idaho State Department of Education
Len B. Jordan Building
650 West State Street
Boise, ID 83720
(208) 334-3475

Illinois
Illinois State Board of Education
100 North 1st Street
Springfield, IL 62777-0001
(800) 845-8749

Indiana
Indiana Department of Education
State House, Rm. 229
Indianapolis, IN 46204-2798
(317) 232-0808

Iowa
Iowa Department of Education
Grimes State Office Building
East 14th & Grand Streets
Des Moines, IA 50319-0146
(515) 281-3245

Kansas
Kansas Department of Education
120 East 10th Street
Topeka, KS 66612-1182
(913) 296-2288

Kentucky
Kentucky Department of Education
Capitol Plaza Tower
500 Mero Street
Frankfort, KY 40601
(502) 564-2983

Louisiana
Louisiana Department of Education
P.O. Box 94064
626 North 4th Street
Baton Rouge, LA 70804-9064
(504) 342-3490

Maine
Maine Department of Education
State House, Station Number 23
Augusta, ME 04333
(207) 287-5800

Maryland
Maryland Department of Education
200 West Baltimore Street
Baltimore, MD 21201
(410) 767-0410

Massachusetts
Massachusetts Department of Education
Quincy Center Plaza
1385 Hancock Street
Quincy, MA 02169
(617) 388-3300

Michigan
Michigan Department of Education
P.O. Box 30008
608 West Allegan Street
Lansing , MI 48909
(517) 373-3310

Minnesota
Minnesota Department of Education
712 Capitol Square Building
550 Cedar Street
Saint Paul, MN 55101
(612) 296-2046

Mississippi
Mississippi Department of Education
P.O. Box 771
550 High Street, Rm. 501
Jackson, MS 39205-0771
(601) 359-3631

Missouri
Missouri Department of Elementary &
    Secondary Education
205 Jackson Street, 6th Floor
P.O. Box 480
Jefferson City, MO 65102
(573) 751-3486

Montana
Montana Office of Public Instruction
106 State Capitol
Helena, MT 59620
(406) 444-3150

Nebraska
Nebraska Department of Education
301 Centennial Mall South
P.O. Box 94987
Lincoln, NE 68509
(402) 471-2496

Nevada
Nevada State Department of Education
400 West King Street
Capitol Complex
Carson City, NV 89710
(702) 486-6457

New Hampshire
New Hampshire Department of Education
101 Pleasant Street
State Office Park South
Concord, NH 03301
(603) 271-2407

New Jersey
New Jersey Department of Education
225 West State Street, CN 500
Trenton, NJ 08625-0500
(609) 292-2070

New Mexico
New Mexico State Department of Education
Education Building
300 Don Gaspar
Santa Fe, NM 87501-2786
(505) 827-6587

New York
New York State Education Department
111 Education Building
Washington Avenue
Albany, NY 12234
(518) 474-3901

North Carolina
North Carolina Department of Public
    Instruction
Education Building
301 North Wilmington Street
Raleigh, NC 27601-2825
(919) 733-4125

North Dakota
North Dakota State Department of Public
   Instruction
State Capitol Building, 11th Floor
600 Boulevard Avenue East
Bismarck, ND 58505-0440
(701) 328-1630

Ohio
Ohio Department of Education
65 South Front Street, Rm. 808
Columbus, OH 43266-0308
(614) 466-3593

Oklahoma
Oklahoma Department of Public Instruction
Oliver Hodge Memorial Education Building
2500 North Lincoln Boulevard
Oklahoma City, OK 73105-4599
(405) 521-3337

Oregon
Oregon Department of Education
700 Pringle Parkway, Southeast
Salem, OR 97310-0290
(503) 378-3586

Pennsylvania
Pennsylvania Department of Education
P.O. Box 911
333 Market Street, 10th Floor
Harrisburg, PA 17126-0333
(717) 787-2967

Rhode Island
Rhode Island Department of Education
22 Hayes Street
Providence, RI 02908
(401) 277-2675

South Carolina
South Carolina State Department of
   Education
1006 Rutledge Building
1429 Senate Street
Columbia, SC 29201
(800) 541-7525

South Dakota
South Dakota Department of Education
700 Governor's Drive
Pierre, SD 57501-2291
(605) 224-6978

Tennessee
Tennessee State Department of Education
100 Cordell Hull Building
Nashville, TN 37243-0375
(615) 532-4885

Texas
Texas Education Agency
William B. Travis Building
1701 North Congress Avenue
Austin, TX 78701-1494
(512) 463-8976

Utah
Utah State Office of Education
250 East 500 South
Salt Lake City, UT 84111
(801) 538-7740

Vermont
Vermont Department of Education
120 State Street
Montpelier, VT 05620-2501
(802) 828-2445

Virginia
Virginia Department of Education
James Monroe Building
14th & Franklin Streets
Richmond, VA 23216-2120
(804) 225-2020

Washington
Washington State Department of Public
   Instruction
Old Capitol Building
Washington & Legion
P.O. Box 47200
Olympia, WA 98504-7200
(360) 753-6775

West Virginia
West Virginia Department of Education
1900 Kanawha Boulevard
East Building 6, Rm. B-358
Charleston, WV 25305
(800) 982-2378

Wisconsin
Wisconsin Department of Public Instruction
125 South Webster Street
P.O. Box 7841
Madison, WI 53707
(800) 441-4563

Wyoming
Wyoming Department of Education
2300 Capitol Avenue, 2nd Floor
Hathaway Building
Cheyenne, WY 82002-0050
(307) 777-6261

State Offices of Teacher Certification

Alabama
Certification—Division of Professional
    Services
Department of Education
Gordon Persons Building
50 North Ripley Street
Montgomery, AL 36130-3901
(334) 242-9977

Alaska
Teacher Education and Certification
Department of Education
Alaska State Office Building, Pouch F
Juneau, AK 99811-1894
(907) 465-2831

Arizona
Teacher Certification Unit
Department of Education
1535 West Jefferson Street
P.O. Box 25609
Phoenix, AZ 85007
(602) 542-4368

Arkansas
Office of Teacher Education and Licensure
Department of Education
#4 Capitol Mall, Rm. 106B/107B
Little Rock, AR 72201
(501) 682-4342

California
Commission on Teacher Credentialing
1812 9th Street
Sacramento, CA 95814
(916) 445-7254

Colorado
Teacher Certification
Department of Education
201 East Colfax Avenue
Denver, CO 80203-1799
(303) 866-6628

Connecticut
Bureau of Certification and Accreditation
Department of Education
P.O. Box 2219
Hartford, CT 06145
(860) 566-4561
FAX 860-566-8929

Delaware
Office of Certification
Department of Public Instruction
Townsend Building
P.O. Box 1402
Dover, DE 19903
(302) 739-4688

District of Columbia
Division of Teacher Services
District of Columbia Public Schools
415 12th Street, NW, Rm. 1013
Washington, DC 20004-1994
(202) 724-4250

Florida
Division of Human Resource Development
Teacher Certification Office
Department of Education, FEC
325 West Gaines St., Rm. 201
Tallahassee, FL 32399-0400
(904) 488-5724
FAX 904-488-3352

Georgia
Professional Standards Commission
Department of Education
1454 Twin Towers East
Atlanta, GA 30334
(404) 656-2604

Hawaii
Office of Personnel Services
Department of Education
P.O. Box 2360
Honolulu, HI 96804
(808) 586-3420

Idaho
Teacher Education and Certification
Department of Education
Len B. Jordan Office Building
650 West State Street
Boise, ID 83720
(208) 334-3475

Illinois
Certification and Placement
State Board of Education
100 North First Street
Springfield, IL 62777-0001
(217) 782-2805
FAX 217-524-1289

Indiana
Professional Standards Board
Department of Education
State House, Rm. 229
Indianapolis, IN 46204-2790
(317) 232-9010

Iowa
Board of Education Examiners
State of Iowa
Grimes State Office Building
Des Moines, IA 50319-0146
(515) 281-3245

Kansas
Certification, Teacher Education and
    Accreditation
Department of Education
120 S.E. 10th Avenue
Topeka, KS 66612
(913) 296-2288

Kentucky
Teacher Education and Certification
Department of Education
500 Mero Street, Rm. 1820
Frankfort, KY 40601
(502) 573-4606

Louisiana
Teacher Certification
Department of Education
P.O. Box 94064
626 North 4th Street
Baton Rouge, LA 70804-9064
(504) 342-3490

Maine
Department of Education Certification and
    Placement
State House, Station 23
Augusta, ME 04333
(207) 287-5800
FAX: (207) 287-5900

Maryland
Division of Certification and Accreditation
Department of Education
200 West Baltimore Street
Baltimore, MD 21201
(410) 767-0410

Massachusetts
Bureau of Teacher Certification
Department of Education
350 Main Street
Malden, MA 02148
(617) 388-3300

Michigan
Teacher/Administrator Preparation and
    Certification
Department of Education
P.O. Box 30008
608 West Allegan Street
Lansing, MI 48909
(517) 373-3310

Minnesota
Personnel and Licensing
Department of Education
616 Capital Square Building
550 Cedar Street
St. Paul, MN 55101
(612) 296-2046

Mississippi
Office of Teacher Certification
Department of Education
P.O. Box 771
Jackson, MS 39205
(601) 359-3483

Missouri
Teacher Education
Missouri Teacher Certification Office
Department of Elementary and Secondary
    Education
P.O. Box 480
Jefferson City, MO 65102-0480
(573) 751-3486

Montana
Certification Services
Office of Public Instruction
106 State Capitol
Helena, MT 59620
(406) 444-3150

Nebraska
Teacher Certification/Education
301 Centennial Mall, South
Box 94987
Lincoln, NE 68509
(402) 471-2496

Nevada
Teacher Licensure
Department of Education
State Mail Room
1850 East Sahara, Ste. 200
Las Vegas, NV 89158
(702) 486-6457

New Hampshire
Bureau of Teacher Education and Profes-
	sional Standards
Department of Education
State Office Park South
101 Pleasant Street
Concord, NH 03301-3860
(603) 271-2407

New Jersey
Teacher Certification and Academic
	Credentials
Department of Education
3535 Quakerbridge Road, CN 503
Trenton, NJ 08625-0503
(609) 292-2070

New Mexico
Educator Preparation and Licensure
Department of Education
Education Building
Santa Fe, NM 87501-2786
(505) 827-6587

New York
Office of Teacher Certification
Department of Education
Cultural Education Center, Rm. 5A 11
Albany, NY 12230
(518) 474-3901

North Carolina
Division of Certification
Department of Public Instruction
114 West Edenton Street
Raleigh, NC 27603-1712
(919) 733-4125

North Dakota
Teacher Certification Division
Department of Public Instruction
600 East Blvd. Avenue
Bismarck, ND 58505-0440
(701) 328-1630

Ohio
Teacher Certification
Department of Education
65 South Front Street, Rm. 1012
Columbus, OH 43266-0308
(614) 466-3593

Oklahoma
Department of Education
2500 North Lincoln Blvd., Rm. 211
Oliver Hodge Education Building
Oklahoma City, OK 73105-4599
(405) 521-3337

Oregon
Teacher Standards and Practices
	Commission
580 State Street, Rm. 203
Salem, OR 97310
(503) 378-3586

Pennsylvania
Bureau of Teacher Preparation and
	Certification
Department of Education
333 Market Street, 3rd Floor
Harrisburg, PA 17126-0333
(717) 787-2967

Rhode Island
School and Teacher Accreditation,
	Certification, and Placement
22 Hayes Street
Roger Williams Building, 2nd Floor
Providence, RI 02908
(401) 277-2675

South Carolina
Teacher Education and Certification
Department of Education
1015 Rutledge Building
1429 Senate Street
Columbia, SC 29201
(803) 734-8466

South Dakota
Office of Certification
Division of Education and Cultural Affairs
Kneip Office Building
700 Governor's Drive
Pierre, SD 57501
(605) 773-3553

Tennessee
Office of Teacher Licensing
Department of Education
6th Floor, North Wing
Cordell Hull Building
Nashville, TN 37243-0377
(615) 532-4885

Texas
Division of Personnel Records
William B. Travis Office Building
1701 North Congress Avenue
Austin, TX 78701
(512) 463-8976

Utah
Certification and Personnel Development
State Office of Education
250 East 500 South
Salt Lake City, UT 84111
(801) 538-7740

Vermont
Licensing Division
Department of Education
Montpelier, VT 05620
(802) 828-2445

Virginia
Office of Professional Licensure
Department of Education
P.O. Box 2120
Richmond, VA 23216-2120
(804) 225-2022

Washington
Director of Professional Preparation
Office of the Superintendent of Public
    Instruction
Old Capitol Building, Box 47200
Olympia, WA 98504-7200
(360) 753-6775

West Virginia
Office of Professional Preparation
Department of Education
Capitol Complex, Bldg. 6, Rm. B-337
Charleston, WV 25305
800-982-2378

Wisconsin
Bureau of Teacher Education, Licensing and
    Placement
Department of Public Instruction
125 South Webster Street
P.O. Box 7841
Madison, WI 53707-7841
(608) 266-1027
FAX 608-264-9558

Wyoming
Certification and Licensing Unit
Department of Education
2300 Capitol Avenue
Hathaway Building
Cheyenne, WY 82002-0050
(307) 777-6261

The Unauthorized Teacher's Survival Guide

By Jack Warner & Clyde Bryan, with Diane Warner

" ... the big-time help a beginning teacher needs."

—Rapport

Real-world advice and encouragement for both new and seasoned educators

Two educators with more than 50 years of combined teaching experience in grades K through 12 have collaborated on the most honest, practical, and helpful book ever written for teachers. From gaining confidence in the classroom to avoiding burnout, this book can benefit anyone who wants to start—or continue—a teaching career.

This book is the perfect companion to *Inside Secrets of Finding a Teaching Job* because once you've found a job, you'll need to know how to cope with the complexities of teaching life and how to prevent "teacher burnout" by pacing yourself over the long haul. You'll learn how to fit in with the staff, manage your time, and successfully juggle a teacher's many responsibilities. It is the most honest, helpful, practical book ever written for new teachers and is being used in Mentor Teacher programs in school districts around the country, as well as teacher education departments at universities and colleges.

Education
6 x 9, Paper, 178 pp.

1-57112-068-8 • $12.95

Available in bookstores everywhere!

Luddens' Adult Guide to Colleges and Universities

A Directory of Thousands of Adult-Friendly Degree Programs
By LaVerne L. Ludden, Ed.D., & Marsha J. Ludden, M.A.

Nearly half of America's college students choose a college after they become adults!

More than 6 million adults are currently enrolled in college—and that number will continue to increase. More than 40 percent of all college students are over 25 years old, and that percentage is growing! This is the book to help adults find their way back to school, with up-to-date information on programs at more than 400 collegiate institutions across the nation.

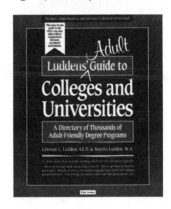

Education/College Reference
7.5 x 9.5, Paper, 576 pp.

1-57112-076-9 • $19.95

Back to School

A College Guide for Adults
By LaVerne L. Ludden, Ed.D.

Inside advice and invaluable information for millions of college-bound adults!

More than 40 percent of college students today are over age 25, and that percentage is far higher for graduate students and part-time students. Adults are going back to school in record numbers. Dr. Ludden, former Dean of Graduate and Adult Studies at LeTourneau University, has written the definitive guide-book on this topic.

Education/College Reference
7.5 x 9.5, Paper, 290 pp.

1-57112-070-X • $14.95

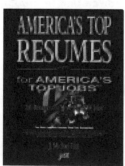

America's Top Jobs™ for College Graduates, 2nd Edition

Detailed Information on Jobs and Trends for College Grads—and Those Considering a College Education

By J. Michael Farr

An essential reference for college graduates, career changers, students, job seekers, employers, counselors, and those seeking upward mobility in their careers.

Not only does this valuable book provide detailed, up-to-date information on 100 of the best jobs for college graduates, it also includes a bonus section containing the best career planning and job search advice available. It contains all the up-to-date and accurate information necessary to identify the occupations with better growth and earnings potential. Use it to help plan your career, education, and job search options!

Business/Careers
8.5 x 11, Paper, 288 pp.
1-56370-281-9 • $14.95

Gallery of Best Resumes for Executive, Management & Other Administrators

A New Collection of Quality Resumes by Professional Resume Writers

By David F. Noble, Ph.D.

From the author of *Gallery of Best Resumes* and *Gallery of Best Resumes for Two-Year Degree Graduates*, comes a book specifically designed for executives, managers, and other administrative types. Again, Dr. Noble invited members of the Professional Association of Resume Writers to submit their most successful designs for this book. The result was the finest advice on resume writing, layout and design that will give upper management (and those aspiring for upper management positions) the upper edge when it comes to selling their skills!

Resumes
8.5 x 11, Paper, 608 pp.
1-56370-483-8 • $19.95

Call 1-800-JIST-USA

JIST Order Form

Purchase Order #: _____

Billing Information

Organization Name: _____

Accounting Contact: _____

Street Address: _____

_____

_____

City, State, Zip: _____

Phone Number: ( ) _____

Shipping Information (if different from above)

Organization Name: _____

Contact: _____

Street Address: (we canNOT ship to P.O. boxes)

_____

_____

_____

City, State, Zip: _____

Phone Number: ( ) _____

Credit Card Purchases:

Phone:
1-800-547-8872
1-800-JIST-USA
Fax:
1-800-547-8329

VISA____ MC____ AMEX____

Card Number: _____

Exp. date: _____

Name as on card: _____

Signature: _____

Quantity	Product Code	Product Title	Unit Price	Total

	Subtotal		
	+Sales Tax Indiana residents add 5% sales tax.		
	+Shipping / Handling Add $3.00 for the first item and an additional $.50 for each item thereafter.		
	TOTAL		

JIST Works, Inc.
720 North Park Avenue
Indianapolis, IN 46202

JIST thanks you for your order!